I Almost Murdered This Child
This Child
[by abortion]

I Almost Murdered This Child
This Child
(by abortion)

Mary Alice McLeod
with Cliff Dudley

New Leaf 🕊 Press
Box 1045, Harrison, Ark. 72601

First printing:

Typesetting by Type-O-Graphics
Springfield, MO 65806

Library of Congress Catalog Number: 82-082017
International Standard Book Number: 0-89221-101-6

CONTENTS

ACKNOWLEDGMENTS

- *Special thanks to my very loving husband, without whom I could not have made it. God knew the special person I needed as a mate and used our love for each other to help us both climb back up the spiritual ladder to forgiveness and growth.*
- Special love to each of our children: Tim, Paul and Anne Marie.
- Special thanks also to our new friends, Cliff and Harriet Dudley. They have been an inspiration to me even in the final writing of this book.

DEDICATION

To my dearest mother,

There are no words in any language that can express my appreciation to you and all you have done for me. I know that I would not have returned to the Lord these past eight years had I not received these things from you in my youth: 1) the spiritual training I received by your motherly teaching and example; 2) your example of physical stamina to hold on when things get rough; and 3) the sense of values that were implanted in my character from babyhood on through my teenage years.

I know you have found it hard to understand some of my actions and will find it hard to believe I could have done the things mentioned in this book; but remember, I am only human and the Bible states "For all have sinned, and come short of the glory of God" (Romans 3:23), and God has delivered and forgiven me every mistake I have made thus far.

One reason our family is growing closer to the Lord every day is because we are trying, with God's help, to be obedient to the Holy Spirit. We may have to give up money, reputation, family or lands. My prayer is expressed in a song that states: "Whatever it takes to grow closer to You Lord . . . " Sometimes it is hard to say that prayer, but I am still saying it. I hope you will have the opportunity to read all the words of that song someday.

I know from my beautiful association with you, that in your spiritual depth, God will grant you the wisdom and understanding to see these things as He would have you to see them. Please know that I love you very much and wish that my life could have been as "pure" as yours from the start, but I am just "me" and had to work out all my problems with God's love and forgiveness.

With all my love,
Doodlebug (Mary Alice)

PREFACE

Over three million babies are slaughtered yearly in the United States. If this book can stop even one such murder and lead a soul to Christ, then no matter what the cost, it will have been worth it.

Richard and I had to weigh the cost in putting these things down for the public to read. I feel like some of the saints of old, that if there is anything I can do or God wants me to do, even if it means rejection, humiliation, criticism, or whatever, if it might save some souls—then I have to write this book. Perhaps I was created for this one thing.

I started this book over five years ago. All along I have fought with the idea of even writing it. It would have been a lot easier not to write these things at all. But the Lord has prompted me along the way to finish it even though I have put it off incessantly. The devil has tried to stop it with great temptations, which, if I had given in to them completely would have destroyed my whole testimony.

Most psychiatrists would categorize me as a severe neurotic with terrific hang-ups in the area of sex, since I made up such wild stories about being raped and et cetera. But the Lord has shown me the reasons that I acted the way I did. I grew up thinking sex was dirty and not wanting any part of it, especially since my natural mother had me illegitimately. To me sexual intercourse was the worst possible thing that could happen to anyone. When I craved an inordinate amount of attention from those I loved and couldn't seem to get it, I proceeded to tell them that the worst thing in the whole world had happened to me—rape.

A few years after my marriage, spiritual healings,

emotional healings, and deliverance had taken place in this realm. God took that tangled entity that was me and straightened it out—again to resemble His likeness that I was made unto. I have asked to be used of the Lord to help others. Perhaps, if they can see that He takes us as we are, if we will let Him, He will change us to be what we are supposed to be.

I sincerely believe that this book is meant to help others who might find themselves in some of the same circumstances. Just recently in my prayer time, the Lord gave me the following Scripture which has prodded me into completing this manuscript:

> "If you wait for perfect conditions, you will never get anything done. God's ways are as mysterious as the pathway of the wind, and as the manner in which a human spirit is infused into the little body of a baby while it is yet in its mother's womb. Keep on sowing your seed, for you never know which will grow—perhaps it all will" (Ecclesiastes 11:4-6, LB).

This verse of Scripture not only inspired me to finish the manuscript, but also confirmed the fact that I needed to include all the material herein, as the reader will gather, as he or she prayerfully reads this book.

—Mary Alice McLeod

1
Meeting My Biological Mother

As I pulled open the heavy door, I saw a woman of small stature waiting in the convent foyer where I had been a nun for almost fifteen years. Her pretty face was aglow with anticipation but apprehension was easily detected by her nervousness.

The steps were few between us, for we couldn't approach each other quickly enough. We embraced and both of us experienced a tremendous surge of love that melted us together as if we were one person. There is no love or closeness between any two human beings comparable to the "mother-child" love. And, you see, thirty-one years had elapsed since my mother had held me in her arms.

Unbeknown to anyone, except for one friend who made the necessary contact for me, she came to see me, never to see me again. But during that one visit so many beautiful things happened. We got into some deep conversation—as if we had known each other every day of our lives. Actually the ties were never really severed.

My own self image was heightened as I spoke with this beautiful, petite lady, and the story of my adoption unfolded before me. My mother was very talented as a dancer and her parents exploited this talent, almost to the very destruction of their child. They sent her far away at the tender age of fifteen to become famous and to make money for the family. No one went with her to chaperone her success adventures, except an agent who introduced her to the gala life of Broadway. Needless to say, she got into trouble.

From the very moment she found that she was going to have a child, she knew she would keep it, no matter what the consequences. Or, at least that is what she thought at the time. I know now that even then in my mother's womb I must have felt this natural and intense love she had for me. I also realize that God's love was upon me from the very beginning of my existence. Surely God's direction was upon my life, even from that time. The psalmist expressed it: "For thou has possessed my reins: thou has covered me in my mother's womb" (Psalm 139:13).

After I was born my mother carried me in her arms many miles South on a bus, crying over me and caring for me as a mother lovingly and dutifully does. She still wanted to keep me, but she had to go back to her family who didn't even know that I existed. Because of fear and the coercion of her mother, she left me in an orphanage on her way home.

A few months elapsed and my adoption was negotiated through the parish priest. He knew about the situation, and also knew a couple who wanted a baby very badly. My natural mother did know who was getting me, and my adoptive parents knew who she was, for they were in the same parish. Both parties vowed never to tell anyone of my origin, especially me. She saw me but could not recognize me openly. My adopted parents did tell me at a very early age, however, that I was adopted. Later on the Lord just opened the doors for me to find my real mother, because in His divine omniscience, He knew that we both had an emotional need to be filled in meeting each other. He also knew that both of us could serve Him better because of that need being filled.

After my adoption, this little lady was counselled to forget about me and to go her way and make a new life for herself. Physically, we were relocated—apart from each other—but for all those years spent apart, we both experienced an intense gravitational pull toward each other emotionally. My psychiatrist said the reason for this was because she had kept me several weeks after my birth.

An inner healing took place, then, after we met—a healing of the harsh disrupting of our natural love and need for each other. In most adoption cases, the baby and its real mother never even see each other. The baby is simply given to its adoptive parents immediately, so that right from the start the child will feel secure with one mother. In my case, even though my adoptive parents were so precious and raised me in a loving home, I did sense a deep emotional tragedy, because my real mother did keep me for a few weeks, and then, begrudgingly, gave me away.

That day when I met her as an adult, I had only two hours to converse with this sweet lady whom I had longed to meet for so many years. I knew then that she never did really give me up. She had always kept up with me from a distance. God had blessed me with some of her talent which I pursued in music. Many times my picture or an article would appear in the local newspaper about my work in sponsoring a musical or broadway play in a local high school. She would see it, clip it, and save it. These things she did in secret, for, to this day, her family does not know about me.

She had named me Ann Marie, and after her marriage, her first child was another girl. She told me that she had given that baby girl the same name that she had given me, trying to fill the void in her life that occurred when she gave me away. I have since then given my baby girl that same name, with a slightly different spelling: Anne Marie. I am hoping that this will be symbolic of a mother-daughter relationship that will never be broken.

Years went by, while she made a new life for herself. I grew up in a wonderful home, full of love, discipline and much overprotectiveness. The overprotective atmosphere was not intentional on my parents' part. Most of it was due to the circumstances like being an only child, and some of it was my fault because I would choose only those encounters that were comfortable to my timid nature. Also, because I was adopted, and by the time I was a teenager and found that I had been an illegitimate child, I somehow got the idea that all sex or any relation with the opposite sex was dirty and to be avoided. I didn't want the same thing to happen to me that had happened to my natural mother. To me, at that time, this meant no association with the opposite sex, even to the extent that I had imposed upon myself a boycott of anyone wearing pants. I would even look the other way when "they" were around, or quickly turn to something else to divert my attention and theirs. Most of the time I used my music as my scapegoat. I practiced the piano for hours—while other kids were out having a good time.

My parents were very proud of me and sacrificed much to give me the musical training that I received. I studied piano with the best teachers available, and even branched out into the study of violin and organ.

The Christian environment in our home was that of highly-structured Catholicism. When I reflect on my early years, I remember that there were times when I felt very close to God, both within my heart and in worship at church. But, somehow this was never a lasting experience. At times, I was very afraid of God. One time I went to Communion during Mass and I had forgotten that I had eaten breakfast at home that morning. This happened when the church still demanded a fast from midnight until you received Communion. After telling mother that I had simply forgotten that I had eaten breakfast, she advised me that I would have to go to confession, and that what I had done was very serious. I trembled, waiting in line to confess my terrible sin. After I told my sins to the priest, he told me that if I ever did that again he would not be able to forgive me. We were taught that the priest was our direct line to God, and that if the priest didn't give you absolution, God was not forgiving you your sins. Later these things influenced my state of mind, when I found it hard to accept God's forgiveness.

The overprotective atmosphere in our home manifested itself in many ways. During World War II, my daddy went into the navy and I was sent to a Catholic boarding school, because there was no one to keep me while my mother was at work. I was in the primary grades, and believe me, this is a very impressionable time for a child. When my daddy came home we resumed a normal family life, but upon entering the fifth grade, for the purpose of pursuing my musical education, I was placed in an all-girl's academy day school. I stayed there until after high school graduation.

The nuns at the school were very sweet and motherly to me. I can see now that I sought this motherly affection from them to the extent that even as a teenager, I stayed at the academy with the sisters almost every weekend—day and night. Neither my parents nor I knew what I was seeking at that time. We had a house at the bay for weekend outings. When my parents would embark on this weekly venture, I would ask to stay with the sisters. I gave my reason as being able to practice the piano four or five hours a day, which in reality I did. But, I was truly in awe of the sisters at work and at prayer. They appeared so happy. I was even allowed to worship at morning Mass with them. There was a peace and security there that I wanted.

Upon completing high school, it seemed to be the thing to do, to enter this Dominican teaching order of nuns that I loved and admired so much. I was really sincere, or at least I thought I was, at the time. I loved God and thought that the convent was where God wanted me. I know now that I made a

Mary Alice, age 1

Mary Alice, first grader

mistake, but God used all those years to prepare me for my true vocation in the future.

I entered this teaching order of nuns at the age of seventeen, and through the years of training in the apostolate and in music education to become a teacher, I somehow lost my first love of the Lord that I once had. At that time the life of a nun was very strict. We were not even allowed to speak until after breakfast. We had to ask for everything. You lived by the bell. We were taught how to practice obedience and humility and were caught up in a very highly-structured life. After a while, I began only to act out the part. I played a superficial role of being a nun. I did all the things I had to do, outwardly, to avoid trouble, but on the inside my life was void and empty. I know that some women find God in the most meaningful way in this walk of life, but I couldn't. I could not be bound by the rule. My spirit cried out for freedom, but I hid these feelings for at least thirteen of the fifteen years I spend in the convent.

I got caught up with my work, teaching school and working toward my degrees in piano. Since the deep spiritual meaning had left my life, I began to seek a new god: music. Music became my idol. An idol is something you worship and seek after with your whole heart. It seemed that my superiors didn't want me to pursue my music. Perhaps they thought that if I achieved a high level of performance, I would become too proud. This made my stubborn nature retaliate by fighting harder to get it. So, while playing the charade of being a nun, I was only seeking a successful career in my music and running away from my inner problems of wanting love and not being able to get it. The Lord loved me so much that He had to chasten me to get me headed in the right direction.

After obtaining my Masters Degree from a very renowned university, I settled down into what I thought would be the answer to everything—the epitome of success—an appointed position as head of a large music department, while simultaneously holding the position of supervisor of music in all Catholic schools in the diocese. I know now that all of this meant absolutely nothing. The Apostle Paul said, "Yea doubtless, I count all things but loss for the excellency of the knowledge of Christ Jesus my Lord: for whom I have suffered the loss of all things, and do count them but dung, that I may win Christ" (Philippians 3:8).

In spite of my outward success, I became more and more miserable on the inside—still starving and searching for something more. You can get lost in your work up to a certain point, but you've got to live with yourself. Depression set in to such a degree that I was finally sent to a psychiatrist. Two years later I finally admitted to myself that I had to leave the convent. I know that all psychiatrists are certainly not good practicing Christians, and not giving the right Biblical advice, but there are a few who have given God His rightful place. The Lord saw to it that I had one of the latter. I spent a couple of years going to him every week.

It was six months before I left the convent when the psychiatrist thought I should look up my biological mother and talk to her. These kind of things don't always turn out good. For some adopted child it could be tragic to find out who the real mother is. But we had already talked about it so much that he thought under the circumstances it might work out. The psychiatrist knew I had this friend who knew my real mother. It was up to my real mother.

She asked her husband, "Honey, do you think I should go?" From time to time there had been some conversation about me. He knew about me before they were married. She perhaps would never have achieved any peace of mind in her longing for me had she not been able to see me. Her husband said, "I think you should go." I admire this man who thought so much of his wife that he put his own family in what might have been a state of jeopardy to allow his wife to see me.

It was about this time of great turmoil in my life that God opened the doors for me to meet my real mother. I was very apprehensive and couldn't think about anything else. I knew she loved me. This beautiful happening aided me in making the decision to leave the convent, for I felt for the first time that I understood myself at least a little. For you see, ever since I can remember, I had compared myself to my adopted mother, who seemed to me to be almost superhuman in every way. I could never seem to measure up to her. But upon meeting my real mother I understood myself as an individual and began to know who I was; and I realized that maybe I was a worthwhile human being after all—just *different* from my adopted mother. I sensed such a kinship of spirits between my real mother and me. She had amounted to something good—maybe there was still a chance for me.

It was then that I knew that I had to leave the convent to find the real me out there somewhere. Of course, when I did finally leave, I was in a spiritual desert. I had achieved a high degree of professional excellence. But I was starving spiritually and hungering for a lasting love that I hadn't found yet, because even though I had met my real mother, I never saw her again. When she reluctantly departed that day, she promised to come sometime and take me to lunch and visit with me, but that never materialized. She was hesitant being seen with me because we looked so much alike. She could not bring herself to tell anyone about me. She was still too embarrassed to face it among her family and friends. After all, her children were grown and they had all made a good life for themselves. Why should something ugly like having an illegitimate child be brought up now after so many years and upset the apple cart? She was very afraid of what everyone would think. I can understand the fear she must have had—the overwhelming fear of what others might think. It can be sheer torture. I, too, have experienced this fear. But the Lord is bringing me out of its clutches as I share my life, the good and the bad, in writing this book.

I do not blame my mother for doing this to me. When she left I thought I would never see her again. I was disappointed, but accepted it because I loved her so much and didn't want to upset her life. I had promised not to invade her privacy. Not only have I forgiven her, but I know it was all in God's plan, for if we had made further contacts I would probably have leaned too much on her in the future.

2
Blisters and Boils

Daddy, going in the navy when I was six years old, necessitated my mother holding down a steady job. This meant that she wouldn't be around to take care of me before and after school. To provide the best care she thought possible she placed me in a Catholic boarding school as I entered the second grade.

Mother's job was only about a mile from the school. Every Friday she would board the city bus which stopped several blocks from where I went to school. She would walk those long blocks, pick me up, and together we would trek back to the bus stop and ride the ten miles on the city bus to our home where I spent the all-too-short weekends with her.

During the weeks I longed so desperately for those weekends to arrive. Every Friday seemed to last about three times as long as any other weekday. The nuns in the boarding school seemed aloof and cruel and to have "favorites" among some of the older girls. All the time I spent there I seemed to be very alone, like someone on a far-away island. As everyone knows, a six-year-old is prone to fantasize from time to time. One Thursday I dreamed up a story of something I really wanted to have happen. I wanted it so badly that I believe I had truly convinced myself that it was going to happen. I told the nun in charge that mother was coming after me on Thursday instead of Friday. Well, when she found that I had lied to her she made me stand in front of all the second graders and chew a bar of Lava soap—actually chew it up—not swallow it—but I had to keep it in my mouth about five minutes. She explained to the class that what I had done was very bad and that if anyone else lied to her, they would get the same treatment.

After the five torturous minutes were over, I rinsed my mouth out time and time again, only to realize that the soreness and blisters that had formed were there to stay for a week. I could only eat very soft food or bland things during that week, and, believe me, nothing special was prepared for me in the boarding school dining room. So, actually, I got very little nourishment for that week.

Not only did I have to endure this physical punishment, but when Mother arrived on the Friday following this incident, to pick me up for the weekend, the nuns refused to allow me to go home as further punishment for my terrible deed. Mother was so disappointed, for she had ironed a special dress for me and polished my white shoes to get me out of the dowdy navy blue and white uniform of the boarding school. After the tiring walk from the bus stop, and bringing my clothes to dress me and take me home with her—she met with this stern refusal. In those days one just didn't argue with nuns or priests. Decisions they made were accepted almost as papal infallibility. So Mother wearily returned home—disappointed and alone.

My weekend was spent not only in physical misery because of my very sore mouth, but even sadder than that, it was spent in the emotional starvation that only a six-year-old can experience. I felt totally abandoned.

Later that year I had the flu, and my sleeping quarters were changed from the common dormitory where everybody slept to a small dormitory—which was called the infirmary. The older girls, perhaps eighth graders, helped the nuns to make beds, gave us our food and changed our clothes. One day one of the girls was undressing me and left me sitting on my bed unclothed from the waist up. She quickly walked over to where some other big girls were chatting with the nun in charge and they all started laughing at me. I heard one girl say, "She has a long way to go before she has anything to brag about." I knew immediately that she was referring to my child-sized under-developed breasts. It didn't take too much sense, even for a six-year-old to figure that one out. I quickly grabbed my sheet and wrapped it around me, which caused even more laughter. Incidents such as this made me overly self-conscious about my body.

The atmosphere was so harsh at the boarding school that we weren't allowed to talk at meals. One day a girl at our table was ill and vomited in her oatmeal. She was forced to eat the oatmeal anyway, while the rest of us gagged as we watched her. There never seemed to be rhyme or reason to the rules or discipline.

In the springtime Mother was called and told that she had to take me to our family physician. I had several large boils on my body which wouldn't heal. Mother was very disturbed about this and immediately made an appointment for me with our family doctor. After examining me, he said the festering boils were a result of poor hygiene. It seems that no one at the boarding school enforced the daily bathing rule with the smaller children, and the large bathrooms were so cold that I had chosen not to bathe—more times than I care to enumerate. Another reason was, I didn't like undressing in front of anybody.

It was not long after this incident that Mother made the decision to take me out of that place and make other arrangements to care for me until Daddy came home from the navy. I suppose the boils were a blessing in disguise, because Mother couldn't take any more of their bad treatment. I don't think that I could have survived in that situation much longer, anyway. A six-year-old child should not have to cope with such abandonment, cruelty, and lack of concern and love.

3
Treasured Encounters

It is true that I did have a deep emotional need to meet my natural mother. That need was filled—it happened in a critical period of my life when I needed some questions answered. It gave me the impetus I needed to step out and start a new life. I wanted to keep up our renewed acquaintance, but she chose not to, in order to protect her family from knowing about me. But I certainly am grateful that the Lord gave both of us that one-time opportunity. I am so glad that her emotional need to meet me was filled also. Just a few years after we met she died of a massive stroke.

A psychiatrist once told me that the woman who cares for you day by day from infancy to adulthood is your mother in a more important way than your natural mother. This lady God gave me to, in this very special way when I was five months old, cared for me every day with much love. And so she is very important to me in many, many ways.

These beautiful adopted parents were the first example to me of God's love that I can remember. There was an abundance of love in our home, so much, in fact, that it overflowed and extended far beyond the realm of the walls of our house.

I will never forget the Thanksgiving Day that we shared our table with two "bums." Daddy was skilled in the cement-finishing trade, and much of his time at that job and commuting to it was spent in the company of men who were somewhat unstable. His path crossed with two such men right before Thanksgiving one year. In talking with them he found that they had no families, or anyone to care for them during the holidays. Daddy asked Mama if she minded if they joined us for Thanksgiving dinner. Her reply was that they were welcome, but that they would have to be clean and shaven when they came to our house.

The festive day arrived with all its grandeur—turkey, dressing, and all the trimmings, yes, even the good crystal, sterling silver and fine china. Mother set a scrumptuous feast before us. There was a knock at the door at eleven-thirty that morning and there they stood. Not only were they clean and shaven, but they must have gone out and purchased second-hand suits for the occasion.

Mother and I tried awkwardly to keep the conversation going at dinner, but it was Daddy who really kept things going in a friendly spirit, with his jolly chuckles and that twinkle in his eyes that could captivate anyone and put him at ease. That day was a blessed one for us. We were blessed by the love that Daddy had in his heart for those two men, who in worldly circles must have seemed as outcasts. Daddy put into practice Hebrews 13:2: "Be not forgetful to entertain strangers, for thereby some have entertained angels unawares."

Daddy was a little on the rough side. He had to quit school after the fourth grade and work with his dad on construction jobs to help support the family. He was a real outdoorsman and a "man's man"—and yet he had the kindest nature. It was portrayed not only in big obvious ways, but even more importantly, in the small insignificant everyday things that really matter more than anything else. He would compliment Mother on every food preparation endeavor, and even helped her many times in doing the cooking and the washing. He never forgot birthdays or anniversaries. So the tender and special times, especially the kind words and affection, made up for any roughness or lack of education that many people believe are threats to one's character or quality of personality.

He made me feel really proud to be his daughter because he complimented me on many, many things. I had endearing nicknames like "Doodlebug" or his "little Dutchman." I was so proud when I was able to help him hold boards when he sawed them or just any small job like that. I felt special just going fishing with him by myself.

Love was manifested daily in Mother's life, also. Her sacrificial love for me was most apparent. She worked and did without many things for herself that I might have the best music teachers available in order to nurture the talent that God had given me. Yet, the most important way a parent can manifest love to a child is how they direct that child to God. Mother has always put God first in her life, and this makes her pretty special to me.

I know God is going to reward her richly for her love of her fellowman too. Once when she had to spend a few weeks in the hospital, an incident occurred that proved this love and concern for people. She was waiting to be checked out in the hospital office when she couldn't help hearing some cruel haggling going on just ahead of her. It seems this young Latin American girl was trying to check out but could not pay any money on her bill. The hospital staff decided to release her as soon as possible, but would not release her newborn baby until the bill was paid in full. Of course, the nursery bill would increase day by day, with the baby still there. The young mother couldn't stand being separated from her baby and was most upset.

Mother was so touched by the young woman's fear and anxiety that she stepped up to the desk and paid the bill for her. The hospital staff retaliated with anger, and even reprimanded Mother with the retort: "You can rest assured that you'll never get a penny of that money back!" Oh, the narrow-mindedness of our cut-throat society! Surely, they had never taken seriously what Jesus said, "As long as ye have done it unto one of the least of these my brethren, ye have done it unto me" (Matthew 25:40).

In coping with the rough and carefree side of Daddy's nature, Mother had to lead a very sacrificial life to keep our home intact. Since Daddy, when he was growing up, didn't have many material things or have much fun as a child should have, sometimes he overspent on things like boats, guns for hunting, etc. But, Mother's sense of values were really in the proper perspective, so she had to sacrifice much to keep her priorities straight. She paid all of the bills and took care of all the financial burdens. Her lineup of priorities went something like this: first, we always had good food to eat; second came my education, which included private schools all twelve years, and my private music lessons in piano, violin and organ, no matter what the expense. Having some type of decent clothes to wear came about third on her list. This really didn't matter to her as long as we were neat and clean. But since I attended the best private school in our city, believe me, the girls there were dressed "fit to kill." But just because I went there didn't mean that I had to match them. At least Mama didn't think so. However, for important things (in her mind, at least) like my senior piano recital, she went to a lot of trouble and spent a lot of money (like $50) just for the material for my dress and another $50 to a seamstress to make it. Special invitations were sent to many friends and special programs were printed.

Mary Alice, at 19, right after receiving black veil in Houston, Texas.

4
The Masquerade

There was no one around in the convent that afternoon as I quickly plunged the huge needle into my finger, knowing that the faster I did it, the less it would hurt. Then, squeezing my finger very hard, I clumsily wrote with my own blood: **I PROMISE MY SOUL TO YOU!**

I had devised this self-appointed ritual in desperation as a bargain with the devil to make me sick so that I would receive extra attention and tender loving care. You see, an emotionally-starved person will do anything to receive love and attention. The devil did not give me any visible sign of his part in this pact. He just sat back and allowed me to wallow in my lies about being sick. He didn't have to seal this pact with any bizarre manifestation, for at that time he had me securely in his grips. He only uses the bizarre things to attract attention of those people who are naive, or are so simple they don't know he is around. To those of us who are clever and manipulative, and somewhat self-sufficient, he already has a foothold—for we have certainly drawn away from God to get that way. Why should he work overtime when he could just sit back and watch me do all his work in my life? What I did was simply an affidavit—a further promise to him—showing him I wanted to keep right on being deceitful or committing whatever sin it took to procure the attention I so desperately needed.

I started lying to get attention in grade school, and as the years went by, the lies just kept on getting bigger—and happening more often.

I didn't delve into witchcraft *per se*—I simply lived a sinful life. It was a sick masquerade. After leaving the convent I did read my horoscope in papers and magazines. It was not until later, when I started going to prayer meetings with my husband, and finally received the baptism of the Holy Spirit that I experienced deliverance. Total deliverance occurred over a period of several years.

Another way this unbalanced state of my personality began to manifest itself was in high school where I found the nuns to be so sweet. Unconsciously, I was trying to substitute them for a "mother figure"—a mother from whom I wanted unlimited love. My adopted parents were very good to me, but I had always been searching (unconsciously) for my real mother because of the circumstances that surrounded the incident where she was forced to give me to the orphanage. I would play sick at school—hoping the nuns would embrace me, love me, or just speak kind words to me—which sometimes they did. But my appetite for love was insatiable. Therefore, the stunts I pulled grew bigger and bigger and more out of proportion.

Before entering the convent we were required to write a letter to the Mother General telling why we wanted to enter the convent. Being smart enough to know what was expected of me, I wrote the right things in the letter, but I don't think an emotionally sick person can be sincere. So my words sounded good in the letter but probably were somewhat shallow in their real meaning. Anyway, I knew they would help me get accepted. I was clever and didn't feel guilty about it.

After entering the convent my lies had become so crafty that many times my superiors were convinced when I played sick that I was really ill. Several times my act was so good that I was hospitalized—even after a doctor's examination. Once it was appendicitis, then for bleeding ulcers, and a few times for other ailments. I never felt too guilty about these trips to the hospital—even though they were launched from a series of lies, because the Catholic hospital where I was sent never did charge us anything, as nuns, for their services. What a way to explain away guilt! Once I was even scheduled for surgery, but after the preliminary hospital tests proved negative, they had to explain away my ailment as something common or trite—like a virus—to avoid embarrassment.

Year after year, one incident led to another, until one time I seemed to go out of my mind—crazy for attention—and proceeded to tell a very good friend (who was also a nun) that I had been raped in an inner city school where I was teaching. Needless to say, she took me in her arms and loved me (feeling sorry for me) and couldn't do enough nice things for me. Wow! Did I thrive (at least temporarily) on all this attention I was getting! But, just as anything is that is sinful, my pleasure was short-lived, and soon empty—gone. My friend was so concerned that she reported the incident to my major superior. My story was proven wrong. As a result of all my lies, I came very close to not being allowed to make my final profession. But, again, I allowed the devil to take over, and by fabrication I convinced my examining council that I had repented and straightened out and was sincerely dedicating my life to the Lord.

Only after meeting my real mother did all this foolishness stop. I knew better all the time. I was not crazy, I had let the devil have a foothold. There was a real need for love in my life that could not be filled in a convent. After understanding myself better, I knew I needed a mate who could love me as I needed to be loved. I needed a lover to share my whole life with, not some substitute who would walk out of the picture after some short-termed incident. Of course, I was totally leaving my need for God out of the picture, even though my deepest need was for Him. At that time I didn't want anything to do with God. I didn't think He cared about me. God did not abandon me through all this. Even though I had promised my soul to the devil in a state of turmoil and confusion—God never turned His back on me. However, I'm sure that this act did enhance Satan's power over my life, but the Lord did not ever turn completely loose of me. He hung in there patiently with me, bringing me out of my dilemma through the years that followed. "Christ died for us even though we were still sinners" (Romans 5:8, my version).

5
Crawfish Pie — Fillets Gumbo

We didn't notice the flat tire until after we drove into the carport. The big Buick held steady all 180 miles back from the bay where we had spent the day. I quickly called my very close friend, who had loaned us the car, and she and her husband came over to the convent to take care of the flat tire.

It had been a splendid day! We had left very early, about five o'clock that morning, for our trip to my parents' home at the bay. Mother had prepared a feast for us, as usual, and we went for a very nice boat ride. This was just one of the many enjoyable incidents that occurred during my four-year stay in Sulphur, Louisiana.

I was still in the long, white habit of a nun, but ever since my new assignment to Sulphur, I had felt half human. When I was first sent there I had misgivings about the place because it was the farthest from our Mother-house in Houston one could be sent, except for California—where we had a few missions. But once there, it didn't take long to find out that our superior was actually a member of the human race. She didn't make you feel ill at ease—like some I had had. If I had a responsibility I didn't have to ask a lot of questions about it or get infinitesimal permissions to carry it out. For a change, we were treated as grown women who had a little common sense of our own.

Our convent was in the second-story building adjacent to the school where we taught. Our building housed the school cafeteria, and right under the convent was the school kitchen, which we used as our convent kitchen, too. It wasn't much to look at—in fact the convent quarters were very small. Our bedrooms were very small, all six of them opened up onto a living room area which was in the center, with a tiny chapel off to one side.

We were out in the middle of nowhere in that little town. Across the street from our school were two little shanties where every fall the folks butchered two or three hogs right in the front yard, the old-fashioned way. They would have a big fifty-gallon drum in which water would be boiling, and the hogs would be strung up over a limb of a tree. They would lower the rope and dip the dead animal in the boiling water and scrape the hair off of it. There was no way a teacher there (at least on the front side of the school building) could keep her class from watching this animal slaughter and cleaning. Annually we stopped class and watched this procedure.

There were only four of us nuns there, and the rest of the eight grades were taught by lay-teachers. Our school cafeteria was manned by very earthy Cajun folks who really knew how to cook. At least three days a week one could smell the aroma of hot yeast rolls all over that school building. We had to cook only our breakfast and the evening meal, for we ate whatever these dear ladies prepared for the school children at lunch time. Their lunches were more like a big dinner, consequently we just had to prepare a light meal in the evening.

I taught private piano lessons after school and had my own music room, with a tiny private bath in it. I enjoyed decorating this room as I pleased. It was my own special territory. How I treasured the freedom that that little room held for me!

In the convent, we were usually allowed to see our family one Sunday afternoon each month. Mother and Daddy made the first long trip from Houston to Sulphur one weekend to see me. Since the trip was so long, they came on Saturday, stayed in a motel, and went back home Sunday afternoon. As long as I live I will never forget their first visit to Sulphur. They were allowed to come over after church on Sunday morning. We had a nice visit in the school cafeteria, where they were allowed to have coffee with me. On visiting Sundays before, for the past seven years, in fact, only the very wealthy parents were served anything. They were taken to private little visiting areas and served coffee and cookies on very fine china, while the rest of us visited in a big public lounge—where our parents were treated in an aloof manner, almost as strangers. We weren't allowed to eat or drink anything with them.

To top it all off, my new superior was so nice that she and another sister prepared Sunday dinner for me and my parents that day. I actually got to eat with my parents!! Daddy was so amazed. He kept saying, "She's treating us like kings." At the other convents where I had been before, Daddy never did feel welcome, so he had stopped coming to see me. But after his first visit to Sulphur, where he felt such warmth, love, and acceptance, he looked forward so much to our visits, and hardly missed one of them.

Mama and Daddy started coming on Friday and spending the whole weekend with me. They still spent nights at the motel, but I had all day Saturday and most of Sunday to be with them. As much as Mother and Daddy both liked to cook, we couldn't keep them out of the school kitchen. They just began cooking for all of us. They would bring special things to fix, and all of us together would have a "ball" cooking, visiting, having coffee—showing our love for each other in Christian fellowship.

I was even allowed to go with my parents to Sunday Mass. They would come from the motel and pick me up and we would drive to the parish church. The other sisters would go in the convent car.

I was not the only nun there who was treated like that. Our superior treated all the other sisters' relatives the same way. She became my very good friend, too. And, of course, she endeared herself so to my parents that in years to come, she was and still is, like a member of my family. When Daddy died, she came to our home and stayed overnight with us so as to be there for the funeral. Even after I left the convent and had a bad car wreck, she came from very far away to take care of me—day and night. I don't believe I have ever had such a close friend. Even though distance and lifestyles have separated us, our spirits are still closely knit together, and she tries to come and stay with me and my family for a week each summer. Big changes might occur in our lifestyles, but our love for each other remains constant.

The lay friends I met in Sulphur were so fine, too. It was there that I first began to feel like an adult and to observe other adult lifestyles. I had entered the convent so young, and hadn't dated except for the junior and senior proms. We now got to go and fellowship with my friends at their homes. Life in general began to feel a little more normal.

The friendship of these friends remained constant through the years, too. A few years after I left Sulphur, when I began to feel unhappy and depressed, they bought me an airplane ticket so that I could come and stay with them for a while. They understood my need to get away, so I could try and get it all together, so to speak. They met me at the airport, and during my few days stay at their home we laughed, cried and prayed together. I dressed as I pleased—in lay clothes. They didn't care, and our rules had relaxed to the point by then, that lay clothes were allowed. We even had a party while I was there. They had a few friends over, served drinks, snacks, and we danced. I forgot about my troubles for a while anyway. These friends are very dear to me, too. Our correspondence has slowed down to maybe a few letters a year, but I know that if I need them, they will be there.

This couple had a widower friend who was very nice, too. I was attracted to him over a span of about three years, although I was not in love with him. I danced with him at the party we had at their house and felt that there was some attraction for me on his part, too. But he was very careful not to overstep the boundaries of proper decorum that he felt about my being a nun.

But I must say, the feelings that I had for him surprised and shocked me. I never thought it was possible that I would have any feelings for a man at all. I guess I thought that I was immune to the natural urgings of man. It probably was important that I went through these "quasi-romantic" feelings, or whatever they were, to enable me to see that I was just an ordinary human being.

6
Reprieve From Routine

Most of the years I spent as a nun were highly structured, which went against my artistic nature, so I was always yearning for more freedom. Well, I got a chance for freedom, so to speak, when I finally succeeded in convincing my superiors that I had to stay on the university campus for a whole year while working on my Masters Degree in piano. This was one of the requirements toward that degree, anyway.

One of the other nuns, about two years younger than I, was going with me to work on a Masters Degree in Business Administration. Our community rented a car for us and we drove, just the two of us, down the road to "freedom"—so we thought—but actually toward a year of unsurpassed heartache and labor.

The university was a two-day trip from our hometown and we stayed overnight in a motel. We were having sensational feelings like shackles being broken from our hands and feet. We had taken the vows of poverty, chastity and obedience, and now all of a sudden we had a car, money to spend, and only ourselves to answer to. The only thing that spoiled our freedom was that we looked so different from everybody else around us. We were still wearing the long habit and people did stare at us quite a bit. One of the fringe benefits of having on that attire, though, was that while we were having our evening meal in the motel restaurant, our waiter brought us the message that our supper had been paid for by a sweet old couple a few tables away from us.

We arrived in the small university town, turned in the rented car, and then settled in at our designated dormitory. We each had a private room, but were not on the same floor—which added to the aspect of freedom—freedom from each other. We never checked on what the other was doing, and were not in the same school at the university. She was in the business school and I in the music school. They were twelve blocks apart.

Having this new kind of freedom liberated me so suddenly—after eleven years of highly-structured life—it had strange effects on me.

The other women who lived all around us in the graduate dorm were living in worlds so opposite to ours. The girl who occupied the room next to me shared a phone on the wall between our rooms. There were tiny doors opening into each room. I used to listen to her talking to her boy friends. What an enlightenment!!! This girl was actually enjoying talking to boys on the phone.

The work at that university was very hard and occupied most of our time. As nuns we were supposed to be self-disciplined enough to go to daily Mass at the local church. This got to be quite a burden to me. The Catholic Church was ten blocks from our dorm, and I just didn't make it to Mass many times. Actually, I had started slipping spiritually three or four years after entering the convent. We were also obligated to recite the Little Office of the Blessed Virgin Mary—a series of Scriptures that took from forty-five minutes to an hour every day. We were also to recite the fifteen decades of the rosary, do spiritual reading, and meditate fifteen minutes every day.

To be truthful, I almost never did these things. I tired of this routine almost immediately after entering the convent.

When I first entered, we had a set routine or schedule for doing all these things together. When the bell rang we went to the chapel like robots and performed these spiritual duties. But when I started teaching school I felt no obligation to make up the prayers I missed during the school day. Really, I just couldn't be bothered. Saying the same prayers out of a book, or from memory, day after day, was a complete bore to me. So I gave myself a private, unorthodox dispensation from these things and didn't feel badly at all about not doing them. When at the university, it was even easier to dodge this routine because there was nobody to check up on me. What bliss!

There were several nuns on campus that year and we chummed around together. Most of us were in the graduate music school and together attended classes, concerts, plays and operas. I also made some friends among the lay people there. Aside from my friends in Sulphur, Louisiana, prior to my university studies, these were the first real friends I ventured out to make on my own, and they were all good relationships. But my hunger for love caught up with me again and the search for it began to manifest its ugly head in two ways that I remember vividly.

I pretended to be ill again. I was aiming at getting the sympathy and love and attention of my piano professor. I drank gallons of water and would not go to the bathroom. Then I would show up at the university hospital and they would have to catheterize me because I told them I could not empty my bladder on my own. The nurse was always amazed that my bladder would contain so much urine. I did this several times, and finally the doctor said I had to spend the Easter vacation in the university hospital for tests. While there I had to remain in bed, with a catheter in me at all times to give my bladder a rest. If I got up to walk around, there was a special way to strap the bag to my leg. Imagine going through all that just for attention!

Just as I hoped he would, my piano professor popped in my room to see me during the holidays, on Holy Thursday.

He also had brought a "dummy" keyboard for me to practice on. The keys moved up and down but it made no noise. He only came that once to visit me—there was nothing to it but a genuine caring type of visit. But I ate it up and liked one aspect of it—he saw me dressed in a gown, housecoat and no veil on my head. I must have actually looked like a normal human being to him.

My companion went to another city for a convention that weekend and when she returned, I had the very daylights shocked out of me. She came in to see me at the hospital just beaming and told me that she had gone swimming on the beach with a priest friend of hers—and that one thing had led to another. I don't know why I thought that what she had done was any worse than what I had done, in all my lying and pretending, because probably deep on the inside, I suppose we were both looking for the same thing—love.

About a month elapsed and I decided to try something else. I showed up for my weekly piano lesson in a very dejected mood. I had decided to tell my professor that I had been raped in the ladies restroom over the weekend, at a time when there were very few people in the music school. I hoped he would put his arm around me, hug me or something. Instead, he just went wild in a kind of restrained way. This story was reported to the assistant dean of the school of music, and one thing led to another. I met with the police secretly at the assistant dean's apartment to give them my story. A few days later I was asked to identify some suspects—which, of course, I couldn't do. Finally the whole thing was dropped. One policeman said it was almost impossible to believe that the rape could have even taken place because sex was so free on the campus, and one didn't have to look very far to find it, that it could be procured very easily. So, why would anyone want to rape a nun, unless they had something against Catholics or the Catholic Church?

In spite of all these deceptions and lies to get attention, I did work very hard and completed all the required courses and memorized all my pieces for my Masters' Recital. When the time came for me to play for the jury examination, which consisted of twelve examining professors, all concert pianists, I checked into a local motel for about a week so that I could eat, sleep and drink nothing but music, undisturbed. I really did well for my jury exam. After passing that, I had to give the actual recital for the public. Mother and my close nun friend from Sulphur, Louisiana, flew in for the occasion. After the evening of the recital, we vacationed around the Midwest area for about a week before they returned home. I still had a few courses to finish and stayed through the summer to do that.

During that summer semester I went to the basement of the dormitory where my companion's room was. I had a message to give her, but she was not there. I decided to leave her a note. I got the maid to let me into her room. To my dismay, I found an ash tray with cigarette butts in it, and quite a few *Playboy* magazines in a stack by her bed. I didn't realize it then, but she too had indeed been searching for something. We both had a God-shaped vacuum that we were trying to fill in the wrong ways—through natural love or whatever. Surely, God would have been the last source we would have looked to at that time, for since we hadn't found a personal relationship with Jesus Christ in the convent (and nuns were supposed to be so close to God!), we tended toward the opposite extremes in our search.

After the summer courses were over I was somewhat anxious to get back down South, especially to begin my new assignment. I was to be the head of the music department at a large Catholic high school. It sounded exciting to me—a new adventure in my search. I thought maybe this was the answer to fill the longing in my heart.

7
A Musical Merry-Go-Round

At last I had achieved the epitome of my dreams. In the community of teaching sisters that I belonged to, I had reached the top of my career—that is, as high as one could go in my situation.

I was placed in charge of the music department of a large all-girl's high school in an affluent section of a very large city. The responsibilities I held there really fed my ego. I was over other teachers in my department whom I had to manage in their respective positions; choral and band director; ballet, piano, voice and harp teacher. The setup was beautiful. I had my own office in the music department, which was away from the mainstream of the school. I was free to organize my day to suit my needs. Music had become my "god" and I was almost totally free to pursue its worship.

During my first year there our community of nuns started to accept some of the changes in the habits we were wearing. I was one of the first to volunteer. Those of us who wanted to, could buy some material and get suitable patterns and make new short habits that would relate more to the dress of the day. I jumped at the chance and got the voice teacher in the music department to sew a beautiful white suit for me. I used a Vogue original pattern and she did a beautiful job. I felt like a teenager when I got my first pair of normal ladies' stockings to wear with my street-length suit. Up to now, with the long white habit we wore thick white stockings and "grandma" type lace-up shoes. With the contemporary garb, we still had to wear a veil, but it was short and our hair could show in the front. And even if I was just a little overweight, and perhaps not very good looking, at least I had very nice thick, auburn-brown hair. And I was proud of it. I enjoyed the compliments I received on my hair.

I got caught up in the musical realm of extracurricular activities that year and pushed my inner needs, that were still very real, into the innermost recesses of my being. The glitter and glamour of producing Broadway plays, involving over a hundred teenagers, was placing a fake icing on the rottenness that was still inside of me. I also got involved in much art work with the scenery, and that allowed me to give vent to some other of my creative urges.

Our auditorium stage was huge. I painted a complete backdrop for one of our musicals all by myself. It was so big that I had to spread it out on the gym floor. I had to finish it on one weekend, so the gym could be used again on Monday for physical education.

Another time, I made, out of papier-mache, a huge golden Buddha for one of our musicals! That musical was a thrill for me. It was probably our biggest production. I hired musicians to play in the orchestra and I got to conduct it. There is absolutely nothing that can compare with the total command or authority one feels with that baton in one's hand—knowing that every second—people are moving like clock work, on stage, behind stage, in dressing rooms and in the orchestra pit, to every cue given by your little fingertips.

It's really strange how I can look back now and realize that even though I was not right with God, He used me from time to time in counselling with those young people. I seemed to know how to give good advice; I just couldn't live it.

About that time I had a deep longing to go to Europe. I talked with our principal and teacher from another school. Over a few months a plan was worked out where we offered to the teenagers in our area a tour of five European countries. The kids would take a humanities course and be able to count the credit toward high school graduation. If each adult who was interested could get eight kids to chaperone, he or she could go free. The kids paid enough to pay our way also.

Six weeks of our summer was spent on the continent of Europe—about six to eight days in each of five different countries.

We spent the first six days in London where there was hardly any cultural shock for we could understand the "natives" and they could understand us. The cheap little hotel we stayed in was a dumpy part of town, though. One day another nun and I decided we wanted to go shopping. We took a walk on the street behind our hotel where there were many little shops. I suppose we didn't look too different from any other women around there—except for the short little veils on our heads. As we were window-shopping, some burly-looking fellows tried to pick us up. We succeeded in getting rid of them and just hurried on down the street. We saw a Pub on one corner that looked empty and decided we wanted a beer. We walked in and asked for two beers in a sack "to go." We were going to drink them in our hotel room. It just so happened that the man working in the Pub was Irish and recognized that we were nuns. He just kept muttering, "I don't think my wee great-grandmother will ever forgive me for selling beer to nuns of the holy Church. Saints preserve us!" But, nevertheless, he made the sale. We went quickly back to the hotel with our precious cargo and had the beer as planned, privately in our room.

On the way over to London, on our non-stop flight, which seemed so terribly long, I had begun to notice a Jesuit brother who was chaperoning some boys. He really wasn't handsome—just cute. He had a nice personality. He was lighthearted, happy, and had a terrific sense of humor. From then on throughout the trip it seemed I was always trying to notice him, pick him out in the crowd, sit by him or whatever.

In London I tried to plan excursions for my girls with him and his boys. Then in Holland, where we stayed on the North Sea, in a beautiful little resort area, I got him to go out with me and my friend to have a drink one night. We were staying in a local boarding school. We caught the bus and went down to the beach and visited some of the sidewalk cafes and then headed back to the dorm. It was just like something a group of teenagers would have done. I guess we were living part of our teenage lives that we had missed earlier.

France was not very exciting to me. Even though I visited all the famous museums in these different countries and saw all the things a tourist is supposed to see, I really didn't see them. I only had eyes for my Jesuit friend—all else passed me by.

Germany was the most fun of all. We stayed in a lovely picturesque village in the Bavarian Alps, and it was there that I had the most fun with him. One day I talked him into going on a mountain hike with just me. I took my veil off and wore long pants and a shirt—which shocked two of the nuns who were on the trip with us. Our adventure on the mountain was perfectly innocent, although I'm not so sure I wanted it to be. We hiked up a mountain, ate lunch in a small cafe and then came back down, admiring all the villages and scenery we saw from that height. It was simply a memorable day.

On another day while in Germany, my friend was sick and had to stay in bed. When I heard he was ill I made sure the coast was clear (all the teenagers were in class) and I went to see how he was. He seemed glad to see me, but there was never any physical contact between us. We talked, laughed and joked and then I went my way.

There were two other incidents in Germany that made a lasting impression on me.

One night he invited me over to meet his Hausfrau and her husband, and they served us a very good bottle of wine. My friend could speak German and we had such a good time just sitting and chatting with those very friendly people.

The other occasion was the day we took all the kids swimming to a beautiful lake in the mountains. I had bought a bathing suit in London and some of us dared to go swimming with the kids. Then we sat around on a blanket in our swim suits, some kids and I, and the Jesuit brother. This was extremely shocking to some of the others. I heard about it later when we returned to the States.

The final destination of our trip was Rome. We stayed in small hotels, three of them, for there were about 160 of us, counting all the teenagers, teachers and chaperones. Our small hotels were just a few blocks up a hill from the Vatican. I guess I was supposed to feel extra holy or something while in Rome. But I'm afraid that my visit there had the opposite effect on me.

For one thing, while visiting the Vatican Museum, all I could think of was, *Why don't they sell all that gold stuff and feed some of the starving people in the poorer countries of the world?* I was a little bitter about this, but then museums and monuments to the dead never did interest me. I like living human beings, and wanted to be a meaningful part of someone's real life.

When we toured St. Peters, which is so mammoth in size that it takes your breath away, I experienced a very strange feeling on the inside. We attended Mass at one of the hundreds of altars. While Mass was going on, I began to think that I was going to be freed from all of this, that I would not be bound by all these traditions anymore. It was as if my spirit took wings and just fluttered somewhere above—in total freedom. I knew for certain, that is, I had a perfect assurance that I would someday leave the convent and go on to something else. I didn't know, then, when or where that would be, but I was certain it would happen someday. That was a very strange thing to experience in the "holy of holies" of catholicism—St. Peters in the Vatican, in Rome.

All too soon our European tour was over and we flew non-stop from Rome back to the States. I was sure I would never see my Jesuit friend again, for he was from Canada and was headed back there. I suppose what I experienced with him was similar to a teenager's puppy-love. Anyway, it didn't take long to get over it, although it felt very intense at the time it was flourishing.

Mother met me at the airport, and after we went through Customs, she took me to her home for a rest. I slept for three solid days and nights on the living room sofa; I was so tired I couldn't move, even to eat. The jet lag, plus all the travelling, had really gotten to me.

After a short stay with her, I had to return to the high school where I was teaching. A few months after getting launched into the teaching year, I began to really get depressed. I was not happy even though I was appointed as music supervisor for the whole diocese, which included many schools that I had to visit, and I had an office in the Chancery Office Building downtown where the Bishop's offices were, and I drove a big car to those schools to supervise their music programs. I guess this proves the old cliche that "All that glitters is not gold." My heart was not in what I was doing, and I finally confided in a close friend. She was a member of the council or ruling body of our community and took my story to our major superior. It was decided that I should see a psychiatrist.

When I heard that I couldn't believe it. I wasn't crazy. I thought only crazy people went to psychiatrists, and, also, I couldn't bear what I thought other people might think. But, anyway under my vow of obedience, I had to go. I continued to see him over a period of two years. He had prescribed an anti-depressant drug for me, and after several months I decided to take the whole bottle full of pills at one time. I wasn't handling my problems very well. In fact, I wouldn't even admit to myself that I wasn't happy. After taking the overdose, I hoped something would change—that I would either die or if I didn't die, some other drastic measure might be taken. It was. My psychiatrist sent me to the mental ward of a nearby hospital.

Since he didn't make hospitals calls, he sent a Jewish doctor who worked at that hospital to see me every day. He would sit in a chair and try to get me to unload on him. One day I finally blew up and cursed him, asking him, "What in the _____ did he expect me to tell him?" After my explosion I began to sob. This is really what he wanted me to do all along. For after that I admitted I wasn't happy and would have to leave the convent. Only two days later I was discharged from the hospital so I could make all the necessary preparations for a new life.

It took about three months to carry out my plans, for I had to visit the Mother General, or major superior of our community, and write a letter to Rome asking for a special dispensation from my vows. Leaving without the dispensation meant excommunication. But during those three or four months I was able to shop for clothes in "living color," and the preparation for my new life kept me going and kept up my spirits.

I never felt so free in all my life as when the day finally came for me to leave. I drove away from that place in my new little Renault car that Mother (who was so understanding) had bought for me.

8
Only Five Minutes to Live

Right after I left the convent I decided to move to Shreveport, Louisiana. I wanted to get away from the large town I had lived in as a nun, mainly because I knew I would tend to lean on the people there, and I needed to make a new life for myself in a brand new place. Mother helped me in finding a suitable apartment and gave me $1,000 with which to begin housekeeping.

Mother lived 180 miles south of where I was getting settled. I went to see her every weekend. I was headed back to Shreveport one Tuesday morning after one of these visits when the following things happened:

I was driving north toward Lufkin, Texas, when a horrible accident happened. It was all so quick that I don't remember every detail about it, but this is how it was later related to me:

An old man was driving out onto the highway from a gravel road. He did look before approaching the highway, but was too slow to get onto it, for on his left was a hill and from that direction a lady in a station wagon barrelled into him, then both swerved and hit me. I was an innocent victim of this terrible scene, and it is a miracle that I am alive to tell about it.

My car turned over three times. It looked like a wadded up piece of paper one might be throwing in the trash can.

I was thrown out of the car, through the windshield, which popped out upon impact, and I landed in a lot of mud. Before being thrown out of the car, though, the steering wheel must have jammed into my left side.

You know how people are. When they saw me in the mud, they wanted to move me. I had nothing to say about it for I was unconscious. But the Lord had this whole thing under control, step by step. I had internal injuries, a ruptured spleen, which was very critical. And there I was on a country road pretty far from any kind of hospital.

Just as the people were trying to move me, a registered nurse stopped, came over and examined me, and said, "Don't move her, for she is bleeding internally and is in shock." Just about then a passenger bus stopped and the driver got out to see what had happened. He covered me with one of the blankets from the bus.

In the meantime, one of the passersby had gone to a little store a half mile down the road and called for an ambulance. It came from Lufkin, Texas. It took forty-five minutes to get there.

Even though I was deep in shock, somehow I answered questions. I gave them the name of the town where mother lived, and for some strange reason I gave my aunt's phone number, not my mother's. So the ambulance rushed me to Woodville, where Mother lived, to the Tyler County Hospital. Someone called my aunt and she got in touch with Mother. I believe God allowed my aunt to tell Mother instead of the highway patrolman or other official. It was a more gentle way of her finding out about the accident—if there can be a gentle way.

I remember one thing about that ambulance trip. The driver stopped suddenly upon entering Woodville and asked some pedestrian where the Tyler County Hospital was. After getting directions, he hastily made a turn and took off in the direction of the hospital. The sudden lunge of the ambulance made me regurgitate a lot of warm liquid, and then I was out again.

When we arrived at the hospital, it really looked like the end for me. The doctor took my vital signs. My blood pressure was just a few notches above zero. I had actually bled to death internally. He told Mother that my pulse was so weak that I would probably be gone within five minutes.

The Tyler County Hospital did not have any surgeons on its staff. There are only a few doctors who live in Woodville who attend to the patients there, and if someone needs surgery, or more intense treatment, they are usually sent to Beaumont, Texas, to a big medical center.

But as the Lord would have it, it just so happened that on this particular day some wealthy woman had imported a surgeon from Beaumont to have her operation in her home town; and he had just finished her surgery and was still in the hospital. No one can tell me that this was not in the Lord's plan for my life at that minute.

The local doctors consulted with him and upon his examining me the surgeon said, "We'll have to start blood transfusions immediately and then get in there and find out what damage there is."

Also, they did not have a blood bank in that little town. But after they found my blood type, they got the ambulance driver to give the first pint of blood. Then they called several other townspeople with my blood type who all *just happened* to answer their phone and came to the hospital immediately to donate blood. They had to do a "cut-down" on the main artery in my right leg for these transfusions because all the veins in my body had already collapsed.

After getting my blood pressure up enough to operate, they did exploratory surgery on me. Two days later, when I awoke, I found that they had removed my ruptured spleen and put in a large drainage tube in my side, because there was such a mess in there, and they expected some of it to still drain while I was healing.

The surgeon the Lord had there that day was the most renowned surgeon of the Beaumont area. He really knew what he was doing.

After several days they tried to get me to walk and I couldn't put my weight on one leg. Then they x-rayed and found that I also had a cracked pelvic bone. I was so critical when they first brought me in that they couldn't do any extra tests. They only did what was absolutely necessary to keep me alive. In fact, I also had a lot of glass in my upper left arm, but they didn't even try to remove the splinters until a few days later.

After the accident I was told that it was a miracle I lived so long with a bleeding ruptured spleen, for over an hour had elapsed before I even got to the hospital. I can see the Lord's plan, step by step, in this whole scene because I don't believe anything happens by accident.

1. He had the registered nurse stop and forbid them to move me from the mud.
2. He had the bus driver appear on the scene with a blanket, which is one of the things that is a necessary treatment for a shock victim.
3. He enabled me to tell them where to take me even though I was in shock and only semi-conscious.
4. He had the best surgeon in the whole East Texas area there—ready to be of service.
5. He had blood donors ready and available to give the blood that saved my life.

I could mention many more ways God had His hand on all of this. I sit back in amazement when I think about it. How He must love me! He was so good not to let me die right then for *I surely would not have gone to heaven.* I had really turned my back on the Lord. I was so tired of acting out the part of a nun for such a long time. I was truly running away from anything to do with religion. Out of respect for Mother, I went to church with her that summer but it meant nothing to me. I even played the organ in church, but that didn't mean anything to me either. God must have saved me that day knowing that He would be able to work His way in my life later.

I stayed in the hospital two weeks and then recuperated with Mother another two weeks. I had to be on my back a lot, because of the cracked pelvic bone and then, when I did get out of bed, I had to use a walker to get around for those two weeks.

I know the Lord had His design in all of this, and I certainly do praise and thank Him for bringing me through it all. God's timing is perfect, and I sensed in my spirit while writing this book, that there had to be a very good reason for detaining my moving to Shreveport. I was in such a hurry. I simply had to be slowed down. I was in such a hurry to get out and meet people and do my own thing. I know now that He prevented me from getting into some deep trouble by moving too fast to be on my own. The physical pain I had to endure was nothing compared to some spiritual or emotional pain the Lord was protecting me from at that time.

9
Tuna Sandwiches "a la Romance"

By September 1, 1970, I was settled in my apartment in Shreveport. Mother helped me buy another car and I was busy trying to get piano students to make enough money to pay my bills.

After my interview with the dean of the nearby college music school, I found that my resumes had done me no good. I really wasn't needed there unless I wanted to do some volunteer accompanying for voice teachers and the opera workshop. I took them up on that because I thought if they could see how good I could play the piano and how faithful I would be to any commitments there, they might hire me some day on the staff. That is exactly what happened. I was hired as a part-time piano teacher at mid-term. And this work, along with my twelve piano students, whom I taught in my apartment, provided just enough funds to live on.

It was hard for me to manage with money because I was not used to handling it, for in the convent everything is provided for you—a home, meals and all your clothes, dentist and doctor visits, etc. So, life and its money deadlines was a whole new ball game for me. I began to share the worries of the world along with its pleasures.

I met quite a few nice people at the college, but most of them were more than one generation younger than I and we didn't have much in common. A few of the teachers in the music school became close friends. One was an elderly man, a voice teacher. I accompanied for some of his students. He became such a close friend that later I asked him to sing at my wedding. I had another of the voice teachers, a woman about my age, over to my apartment and we shared a lot about our lives. Later, I grew to dislike her, for she seemed to have unalterable ambitions and would step on anyone in her way in acquiring them.

Sometimes I would go to the college earlier than rehearsal times, so I could practice on the piano that we were going to use. I enjoyed playing on the nine-foot grand so much that one excuse was as good as another to get to do that. One of those mornings that I went early, I ran into the college piano tuner and his wife. His wife went with him everywhere because he was blind. She was his chauffeur and constant companion. I introduced myself to them and found them so real and down-to-earth—such nice people.

After second semester was well on its way I decided to have the college piano tuner and his wife over to my apartment to tune my piano. I had a smaller grand piano which my mother had helped me to get. We bought it in Beaumont, and had it delivered all the way to Shreveport. It was so pretty in the bay window of my apartment, which was on the ground floor. Believe it or not, I never got any complaints about noise from the piano lessons or even my own piano practicing—which I sometimes did for several hours each day.

On the afternoon the piano tuner and his wife arrived, I had purchased a nice coffee cake, and after he tuned my piano, we had a nice warm visit. I jokingly asked them if they knew an available man about my age to whom they could introduce me. To my surprise, they did know such a person. He was a friend of some friends of theirs.

A day or two later I received a call from them. They had

gotten together with their friends and invited the man over to their house the next Sunday afternoon for a light supper—tuna sandwiches. They invited me over so that I could meet him.

I couldn't wait for Sunday to arrive. I got my hair done and wore the nicest casual outfit that I owned. Finally, it was time to go and I drove to their home, which was in a poor section of town. But, everyone there was so nice that the surroundings really didn't bother me. I don't remember who got there first, Richard or I. Anyway, the "vibes" were right, and after eating sandwiches and having a lot of small talk, he invited me to go with him for an ice cream cone. He had a new blue Volkswagen. He was very proud of it. We both seemed to be quite at ease as we made our little trip to the ice cream store and back. I drove home after that short little date and thought, *Well, that's that. I'll probably never hear from him again.*

The next day was just another work day, but as soon as I got home the phone was ringing. It was Richard. He wanted me to have dinner with him. This was the first of a series of uninterrupted consecutive dates for the next two weeks. One night it was the symphony. One day it was a picnic out by the lake. One night it was a movie, and one morning it was breakfast, and so on and so on. Not only did he call me every day but he started calling me every morning as soon as he awoke. He couldn't seem to see me enough.

My mind was in a complete whirlwind, ecstasy, at the thoughts of having someone that could love and care for me, take me to so many fine places. It was almost more than my mind and heart could bear. However, in all this I was very much aware that Richard seemed a little more than hesitant to touch me and I wondered why. Oh, how I wanted to be touched and caressed and kissed. It seemed every feeling within me had been suppressed, and now I wanted to give way to these feelings and to experience for the first time in my life what it was to be a woman held by a man, to know the ecstasy of romance.

One night we went to a movie, and I sat there. Oh,

how I wanted him to hold me and take me in his arms. Finally, I could not stand the pressure of not being touched any more and I reached over and took his hand. As I felt the warmth of his hand, I knew I was in love. That was the beginning.

I realized the reason that Richard was so hesitant about touching me was that I had shared with him my complete story about being a nun. After that night at the movie, however, when I had made the first move that was Richard's "green" light. It didn't take long before all the physical manifestations of our love were in full rage.

Two short weeks after I had met Richard we became engaged. He invited me to go to very high-classed restaurants. "Mary Alice," he said, "dress up real special. This is going to be the 'night' of our lives."

He picked me up and our first stop was to his apartment where I was to meet his landlady and the lady who lived next door. I had a strange feeling. It was almost as if I were being introduced to his family. After having a short visit with these two friends of his, we got in the car and left and started driving to the restaurant.

Suddenly Richard turned to me and right out of the blue said, "Mary Alice, I love you so very much." I waited for something else to follow, but that's all the conversation we had at that time. I wondered, *Why did Richard say that? What does he have in mind?*

Soon we arrived at the restaurant. We had an elegant steak dinner and everything that went with it. Then we went into this beautiful fireside lounge for Irish coffee. Then again, with no advanced notice Richard turned to me and asked, "Mary Alice, what do you think about going with me to buy a marriage license on Friday after work?"

I thought I would fall off the chair. My first thought was, *This certainly isn't the usual run-of-the-mill proposal, and not as romantic as I would have liked it to have been,* but I knew what he meant. My answer was simply, "Yes, Richard. Let's do that. I would like that."

After two Irish coffees, Richard felt like celebrating some more and so did I. We went to the Bossier Strip to a nightclub known for its female piano player. By then I was really feeling good on the Irish coffees. It was around one o'clock in the morning—and after one more drink I played the piano in that bar. There were very few people there, but I still can't imagine that I would ever get the courage to do such a thing, but I did.

Then the regular pianist played some requests for us. It was our night in every way. It was a night of happiness!

After our moments of fun and celebrating, well into the night, Richard drove me back to my apartment. By now we were both feeling very good. He escorted me to my apartment and came in long enough to give me a goodnight kiss. Oh, the warmth of that kiss! As he was about to leave I said, "Richard, please don't go. Stay with me." We were both so starved for love for such a long time that it didn't take very much persuasion on my part to convince him to stay, and it was on that night that we decided to live together. We were engaged but not as yet married.

Instead of our getting married right away like we had planned, we gave in to Mother who wanted her daughter to have a large church wedding. That would take several months to prepare. We were still waiting for our dispensation from my vows—especially the vow of chastity. However, a piece of paper with the seal of the Vatican on it could not keep us apart. I don't think even at that time God could have kept us apart. We were determined to live together. Of course, neither Mother, nor anyone else, knew about our premarital relationship. Therefore, she went ahead, and I went ahead, and planned a big wedding—white dress and all. I continued so cleverly and kept everything hidden from her.

Richard and I knew that what we were doing was wrong and that it did not meet with the approval of the church or God, but neither of us at the time were living for the Lord. We were not strong enough to withstand the temptation that was before us—therefore, we succumbed.

From the very first day that we had met, Richard and I knew that we were meant for each other. As time went on, we knew that the Lord had saved us and prepared us for each other even though God certainly didn't approve of our living together and our relations before we were married. All of the love and attachment that we had for each other at first was just the normal, human love that most people feel when they first fall in love. I know now and I certainly do give God much praise for sending Richard to me, even though he was not walking close to God when we met. He had backslidden and was in somewhat of a depressed state caused by his constant loneliness.

Richard had received the baptism of the Holy Spirit before we met, but if he had told me anything about a Pentecostal-type experience at all, you can rest assured that I would never have associated with him any further than the day that we met. He was the tool that God used to bring me to my senses spiritually. You see, God can use this natural affection of love and turn it around, set it in gear toward the Creator, Jesus Christ.

Our love for each other grew more and more as we sought a romance with God, which should have been there in the first place. My emotions were becoming focused in a proper balance. My psychiatrist told me that this had to take place before spiritual growth can occur. Maybe they began simultaneously. Little did I realize that the chain of events that were to follow would be life-changing, threatening, fearful, and yet the very things that would bring me into a personal relationship with Jesus Christ.

10
Staying the Hand of the Destroyer

Do not [earnestly] remember the former things, neither consider the things of old. Behold, I am doing a new thing; now it springs forth; Do you not perceive and know it, and will you not give heed to it? I will even make a way in the wilderness and rivers in the desert.

Isaiah 43:18-19, *Amplified Bible*

There may be many glamour spots in New York City, but all I saw and felt was mass confusion in the crowds, cold aloofness in the populace of a steel and concrete jungle, and the dingy overcrowded atmosphere that pervaded around the buildings that were supposed to be so attractive.

I wandered with the detached feelings of a stranger to the clinic I had read about in a current women's magazine. An overpowering self-pride had blocked any sense of guilt attached to my decision—and my heart was certainly likened to the cold-heartedness which I felt all about me. My intellect was very confused; as it only counted the cost of my own self-image. Spiritually I had reached the bottom of the ladder where a person puts him or herself first in every situation, no matter what the cost. In this case, it was the cost of a life; the life of my unborn child.

Yes, the respect of other people meant more to me than anything else. It was bad enough for someone else to experience getting pregnant before being married, but for me it seemed a million times worse. So many people, almost everyone, knew that I had been a nun. How then could I live with the fact that I would have a child seven months after we were married?

We were engaged before this child was conceived, and my husband really did want this child of ours. But, still I couldn't cope with the situation, no matter what. I was so afraid of what people might think. This whole incident reminded me of the fear my natural mother had concerning the fact that someone might find out that I even existed, since I was born illegitimately.

I was working as a secretary that summer for an insurance agent when I suspected being pregnant. Richard and I had been living together ever since our engagement. I didn't tell him until after I had seen my doctor and confirmed my fears by the usual test. I recall the afternoon that I broke the news to him. I got home from work first and fixed him a Scotch and water in a very big glass. I had made some kind of hors d'oeuvres for him to nibble on as he had his drink. Before I told him I waited until he had downed at least half the drink, or until I thought he would be relaxed and feeling good.

When I felt that Richard was relaxed, I sat him down. With my heart beating so hard and fast that I thought it would explode out of my chest, I feared his reaction—would he leave me, would he understand—finally, I mustered the courage and said, "Richard, you will not believe this, but I am pregnant."

"You are what?" he asked.

"Yes, I've been to the doctor and I am pregnant."

"That's wonderful, Mary Alice," he replied. "I've always wanted to be a father. I'm so happy."

"You're what?"

"I am. Yes, I'm happy. Aren't you?"

"Richard, did you hear me? I'm pregnant."

"I know it. I want to go tell my dad. I want to tell everyone."

"Richard, we're not married yet!"

"But we will be. I love you. I'm not ashamed. Isn't that enough? Let's tell everyone."

I begged him, "Richard, don't tell anyone. Don't breathe a word of this to anyone." He agreed. Somehow then I seemed to live with the fact that I was pregnant before our marriage. Knowing how Richard felt didn't help. He really wanted the baby, but the entire ordeal was affecting my nerves. I got upset over the least little thing and would fly off the handle. I couldn't bear the fact that I was going to take a marriage vow while I was pregnant. I knew I was going to have a nervous breakdown.

Our marriage was on a Saturday. I had asked for time off from work on Friday to get my hair done. My boss had graciously said yes, but all the time I thought that he should have given me the whole day off before my wedding. After all, I thought, *You only get married once in your life.* We had only planned a two-day honeymoon.

I had so many things to get ready for the wedding. When I went to work that Friday I found that my boss was going to be out of town all day so I just went back home. After all, I was expecting all kinds of out-of-town relatives and there was so much to do.

The wedding took place as scheduled, but I can tell you the devil certainly robbed me of every moment of happiness of that day because I was so worried about the benefits that I would be reaping of having had premarital sex. As I slowly walked down the aisle, and as the vows were taken I thought, I'm lying. This isn't true. There is cause that I shouldn't be married, and all my joy was gone. The gloom and cloud of my pregnancy erased any joy which should have been. However, I put on a good act. No one knew that the joy I should have had simply was not there.

Our one-night honeymoon was spent in a local motel.

That too, to me at least, was almost empty, or meaningless, no joy. There was nothing new. I didn't come to my husband as the virgin bride. We'd experienced it all before. It left me empty, blue and forlorn. Why, oh, why couldn't I have waited? Why couldn't we have waited? That was the question now that I could not answer. I would never know the joy of coming to a husband as a virgin. Why, oh, why, did I make that mistake?

To make matters worse, when I went back to work on Monday my boss called me into his office and really tore me apart for taking the whole day off on Friday. "Mary Alice," he said, "I've grounds for firing you, but because you are such a good employee, I'll give you a second chance."

I sat there listening and agreeing with him, but on the inside I was angry, crushed. I suppose here again everything seemed to upset me far more than I would have been normally—the pregnancy, my worry about it seemed to unbalance my nerves.

When he finished his correction speech, he went out of the office on some business. I was so upset that I walked out right behind him for good. I told the other girl working there that I was quitting. When I told Richard how I had quit he wasn't as understanding as he was on the day that I told him about the pregnancy. He knew that we couldn't afford to live on his paycheck alone, but he did try to understand when he realized how upset I was.

Being without work gave me far too much time to think, and Satan did his job. After being home a few days and this constant twenty-four hour thinking, I became depressed beyond what I can describe in words. I was so ashamed, and I was so afraid of what everyone would think when they found that I was pregnant, especially my mother.

We were married only one week when I found an article in a magazine about abortion clinics in New York. I went to see the doctor and had him fill out the papers that I could take with me. I had decided that abortion was the only way. I had to abort this child to save my face. I borrowed the necessary money and as quickly as I could, made the arrangements to fly to New York City.

Like all newly-weds very much in love, Richard wanted to make me happy no matter what the cost. He wanted the baby. He wanted me to go through with the pregnancy, but yet he didn't stop me from making my plans. He stood by and watched from a distance—not really understanding at this point. I knew that he was totally baffled.

I went to the airport. Every step that I took I realized that I was committing myself further and further into the agonies, fully realizing and understanding that I was going to commit murder. My eternal state hung in the balance. I knew full well that murderers could not enter the kingdom. Yet the price, the shame that engulfed me was even greater than that of eternity. I took a deep breath and boarded the plane. I prayed and wept, yet I was determined that I would go through with the butchering of my unborn child.

By the time I reached New York my mental state was dazed. I was walking somewhat like a zombie. I arrived at a somewhat nondescript facade of a building. I was going in along with several other women. We went inside and verified our appointments at the reception desk. I had to sit in the waiting room for several hours. Even though my heart was still so very cold, and my will so determined, I couldn't help observing those around me. They, like myself, seemed to be in deep, deep depression. Most of the girls that were there with me seemed to be very young and far more afraid and upset than I.

We all waited with apprehension and fear. Many of the others had already undergone the tremendous experience and were waiting for transportation home. A terrible cloud of gloom encompassed everyone there. It was written on their faces. You could feel it in the air. There was total despair. Without exception, everyone was affected.

The nurse then came and took us in groups of four in an elevator down the hall. There were metallic squeaks and groans of the elevator penetrating a thick silence which hovered around us. Being in that place and going from one floor to the other, one suite of offices to another, was like being in some sort of maze in the pits of hell.

Suddenly the eerie and death-like feeling came upon me. There was some strong possibility that one would never find her way out of this place of horror. They had routine lab tests, vital signs were taken, papers were filled out, even a private interview with some sort of counselor—if that's what one could call it. Then the moment finally arrived when we were taken singularly into the treatment room as they called it. We changed into a surgical gown and awaited the death sentence.

As I sat there my whole life went before me. The fear of God, what would my mother say, what would Richard say, what would anyone say if they knew at this moment where Mary Alice McLeod was—in the butcher shop waiting to murder her unborn child? At that point I couldn't have cared less. I wanted the thing to be over with, as quickly as possible. I wanted to get it over with so that I could return home.

Then, as suddenly as a summer storm, there was divine intervention. It was like what was written in Second Samuel 24:16: "And when the angel stretched out his hand upon Jerusalem to destroy it, the Lord repented him of the evil, and said to the angel that destroyed the people, It is enough: STAY NOW THINE HAND!"

Upon examination there was some discrepancy in the length of my pregnancy. The doctor in Shreveport had said it was twelve weeks along, and now the doctor in New York said it was fourteen weeks along. I also had a fibroid tumor, which would complicate any type of abortion. "Mary Alice," he said, "you're too far along for such a type of abortion process as we perform here at the clinic. You will need to go to a regular hospital to have it done another way."

I couldn't believe my ears. I know that the Lord did stay

this horrible thing that was about to happen. He stopped it. It would have been a terrible punishment, just as the angel was dealing with these punishments to Jerusalem. My family and I would have to suffer a terrible punishment had I gone through with the abortion. I knew that I had committed that deed already when I decided and willed to have it done, but I am also of the firm belief that nothing happens without the Lord allowing it to happen. He has control over our lives. Yes, even life and death, and I know the Lord allowed the circumstances to be such, that a halt was put to this deed that I had so willingly wanted to commit.

It was hard to imagine people like those who were in that clinic. The workers there were so sympathetic with my decision to have this thing done that they actually went out of their way to find another possible loop for me to get it accomplished. Even though I knew God was dealing with me, I was still determined to go through with it.

I was sent to a hospital which existed for the sole purpose of abortion, especially the saline type of abortion. I had brought enough money with me to do this. It meant that I would have to stay in the hospital overnight, but I was determined to go through with it, God or no God.

Upon arriving there, I gave the receptionist my folder and I was ushered into a waiting room to wait. Then a very strange thing happened. I waited only for about five or ten minutes and something made me bolt out of my chair. I rushed to the receptionist and said to her, "Discard my folder. I've changed my mind." I seemed to be in a stupor, my mind was foggy—it was as though I had no control over what I was doing. I rushed out of the hospital immediately, only to wander down the streets of New York City, not even knowing where I was going or what I was doing. I ended up in a small coffee shop. It was as though I had no mind or heart, only the actions of a programmed robot. I ordered coffee and a roast beef sandwich. I was sitting there eating it and not even realizing that I was eating.

I then went out to the street and hailed down a taxi and told him to take me to the hotel that I had near the Kennedy Airport. I had to wait until the next day to fly back home. I called Richard that evening and told him that they could not perform the abortion because the pregnancy was further than we had thought. I could tell that Richard was relieved because of his reaction, which was: "Honey, I'm really sort of glad."

I don't think I'll ever forget those words. There were other things that we said to each other over the phone. After I hung up I wept because I knew that God had given me such a wonderful husband in Richard. I couldn't wait to get home to be with him and have him engulf me in his protective arms. At the time I certainly wasn't thinking of the protective arms of God, but oh, how His almighty arms must have encircled me in their protecting love because of the precious cargo that was within me and had been entrusted to me.

The next morning I could hardly wait until my flight was called. What a difference there was in boarding this plane returning home than there was when I boarded the plane in Shreveport. There was joy as I departed from that return flight and rushed into the arms of Richard, knowing that I was going to give birth to our first child. Oh the joy that was in my heart when I realized that Richard and I were going to be parents—and I was going to be a mother.

How I thank God that He loved me enough to stay the execution of my son.

Now our precious Paul is the result of all of this. He's ten years old now and so very dear to us. He is surely God's gift to us in more than one way. The Lord really has had His hand on Paul from the very beginning.

One of the most intense concerns in writing this chapter was how it would affect Paul now and later, should the Lord tarry. I don't want him to think he wasn't wanted, because we love him so much. After seeking the Lord in much prayer and fasting, God has assured me that this will not happen. Paul will not feel this way. For a child his age he already has deep spiritual insights, and I know that he will understand the whole thing as the Lord will have him understand it. He will be able to understand the beauty of God's love for him in sparing him and in using the whole thing to bring us closer to God. How special he really is! I just didn't realize that what I was going to destroy was the precious little Paul that we now have.

I know our marriage would not have lasted if the abortion plans had been carried out. We would have had severe feelings of guilt. Our family would not have grown in the precious Spirit of the Lord. The whole picture would have been one of total disaster. I know that I could not have lived if I had done this thing. Now it is all washed away in the blood of Jesus. I cannot deny that this sinful incident happened in my life, but I also do not doubt the cleansing power of God. **God is bigger than any sin. No sin is too great for Him to forgive.** He has not only made me whole, but has made our family, now a beautiful number of five members, His brothers and sisters and joint-heirs of God's kingdom.

It's not easy to admit that at one time we were in this kind of a pit of hell, or whatever you want to call it. But if God can use this story to witness His saving power to others, perhaps in similar circumstances, I have to say the cost is not too great. I have this great feeling in my spirit that souls are in the balance. This problem of abortion is so rampant throughout our land and throughout the whole world, even to the degree that those on the devil's side are so outspoken about it—and even openly admit that they did this—because a baby would get in the way of their lifestyle. God wants some of us on His side to give witness to the fact that it is a horrible thing, and perhaps this book will give that witness.

It baffles me that God never forsook me through these things. When I was in high school, I did a term paper on *The Hound of Heaven,* by Francis Thompson. Part of it reads:

**All which I took from thee I did but take,
Not for thy harms,**

But just that thou might'st seek it in My arms.
All which thy child's mistake
Fancies as lost, I have stored for thee at home:
Rise, clasp My hand, and come."

Halts by me that footfall:
Is my gloom, after all,
Shade of His hand, outstretched caressingly?
"Ah, fondest, blindest, weakest,
I am He Whom thou seekest!
Thou dravest love from thee, who dravest Me."

In high school I was searching for a real, personal God in writing that term paper, and now I feel compelled to refer to it—finally realizing what this search was all about. I left Him (God) many times and sought Him unknowingly in many wrong things, looking for His love, but He was and is like the HOUND OF HEAVEN, constant in His search for me. He has never given up on me.

As far as I am concerned, this miracle, out of all the great big ones the Lord has done for us, the stopping by divine intervention of this dastardly deed is the biggest thing the Lord has ever done for me and my family. *It was the turning point spiritually in our lives*—especially mine. After this incident I was led to seek forgiveness, then the Lord could really begin to work with me and my family. So you see, I could not leave out this sordid, ungodly action on my part. This book is to give glory to God and to win souls for heaven and not to just simply paint pretty pictures of me or my family.

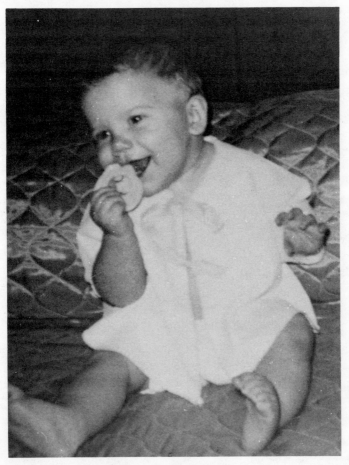

Paul, age six months

11
A New Confrontation

Late one afternoon, several months after we were married, Richard said he wanted to go to a prayer meeting. My reaction was one of total dismay. I asked, "A what?" Well, there I was at home, feeling sorry for myself in my pregnant state and wishing for Richard to be there with me and not off to some kind of meeting of religious fanatics.

You know how lengthy some prayer meetings can be. The longer he stayed, the more upset I got. I could not understand Richard's actions at all. I felt he should be home sitting with me, holding my hand, and watching television with me, or us doing something together.

The Lord broke me in very gently and slowly, though, to this new kind of religious experience. Richard never did force any of it on me. He went to these prayer meetings only a few times while I was pregnant.

I was teaching piano up until about the ninth month of my pregnancy. It just so happened that one of my students was a dentist's wife who knew all the answers to everything, especially in the medical realm. I had started teaching her piano before I met Richard, and she and I had become good friends.

When the time approached for our baby to come, she and I had concocted a way to let my mother surreptitiously know the good news. Mother thought the baby was due in April—or so we told her—but in fact, the due date was in February. I had told her this because I still could not own up to the fact that Richard and I had lived together before marriage and this child was in fact conceived two months before we were married. My doctor had told me that the baby would have to be a C-section delivery because of my fractured pelvic bone, an injury from the car wreck. Well, in talking with my friend, the two of us used this C-section delivery as the base for a gross lie to tell Mother. She planned to call Mother for me and tell her I started hemorrhaging and that they had to take the baby. The night I checked into the hospital my water broke, and Paul had to be delivered by C-section—about 3:30 in the morning. This fact helped to solidify the story that we planned to tell my mother.

As the birth trauma unfolded and I had this child, I felt very distressed. I tried to be a good mother—whatever that is supposed to be—and found it very hard. I had tried to nurse Paul but couldn't. The problem being that one of the nipples was inverted and he couldn't suck. We tried for two days. He lost nearly a whole pound in weight before leaving the hospital. I felt like he was a threat to me in some ways. On the inside, I didn't feel good enough to be entrusted with one of God's special creations. I was almost afraid to love that little child at first. As I held him in my arms he was just like a little doll. Bringing this beautiful little child home from the hospital was such a lovely experience though. Oh, the wonderment of it all! Day by day I watched his little personality develop. I couldn't help loving this tiny, helpless little boy. My love for him grew more each day as he took on the characteristics that make up his own individual personality. Then I knew how precious a baby he was. Yes, I have a special love for this child (as I do all of our children). I hope he can forgive me for almost murdering him through abortion. I hope he realizes that God loves him so much that He spared him through the circumstances that existed. God must have something very unique in store for him.

We had made a mistake in living together before marriage, and I wanted to blot out the mistake. But lies don't cover up anything; only forgiveness from the Lord can wipe the slate clean. After sincere repentance, God turned my mistake around and gave Paul to us. What a blessed treasure this child is!

More and more I realize the goodness of God. I got down on my knees and asked the Lord to forgive me, and cried bitterly for what went on those years. I embraced the foot of the cross and wept so hard that I was shaking all over—that's when I really met Him as my personal Saviour. I had accepted Jesus as Saviour as a child, but He certainly wasn't Lord in all areas—He was like the Old Testament God that you approach with fear and trembling. I was so guilty of thinking I had to work for my salvation.

About six months after Paul was born I tolerated going to prayer meetings with Richard once in a while. Then they became more frequent—until we found ourselves going to them every week. By that time I could tell that these meetings meant a whole lot to Richard, and I loved him so much from the very beginning of our relationship, that anything he wanted to do I wanted to do with him to make him happy.

Many months went by and many prayer meetings went by, and according to all outward appearances, I know I seemed to be spiritually immovable. But inwardly, the Lord was preparing my heart to meet Him again in an even better way.

On Easter Sunday, 1973, a friend of ours went with us to the hospital to minister to Richard's mother. Upon returning to our home he was led to pray for me to receive the baptism of the Holy Spirit. I did experience a new kind of peace, but there was no evidence of speaking in tongues at that time—this was to come later.

In the summer of that same year we spent our vacation in South Bend, Indiana, at the Catholic Charismatic Conference at Notre Dame University. While there in that enormous football stadium, with forty thousand other believers praising the Lord, I was overcome with the power of the Holy Spirit and began to sing in a heavenly language. I knew, without a doubt, that the Lord Jesus had begun some very special work in my life. It was new and different and very refreshing. I certainly hadn't expected what I was feeling.

I had gone so far downhill spiritually that there was no communication with God for a long time. I believed that God would not forgive me for all my wrongdoings, and therefore for Him to love me was just not possible. But this infilling with the Holy Spirit spun the old man in me in the direction of a complete about-face. I supposed when the minister prayed with me on that Easter Sunday, forgiveness came then, for I experienced great peace. But now at Notre Dame came the fullness of the baptism of the Holy Spirit. I experienced so much love—much, much of God's love. I was totally overwhelmed and couldn't stop praising God for His mercy and love toward me.

This experience could not be compared to any previous religious experience and, believe me, I had undergone a lot of religious experiences. When in the convent, I went through the very moving ceremony of the postulant. This is when a girl who has just entered, after being observed for nine months in a training program, receives the religious habit, or garb of a nun. The girls walk down the church aisle, dressed as brides, typifying their total dedication or the giving of themselves and their lives to Christ. During the ceremony, they leave the chapel, don the religious habit and return dressed as nuns. Truly, this is a beautiful ceremony. And even for me, at that time, it was very meaningful. You see, I was still dedicated to the Lord, and I thought I was seeking Him in the right way at the time of receiving the habit.

After wearing the white veil of a novice for a whole

year, and pursuing further theological studies, the day approached when our group would make temporary vows—for one year—the vows of poverty, chastity and obedience. These are made to God in a very beautiful ceremony. While kneeling before the altar, the novice becomes a professed sister. She then receives the black veil. The vows are then renewed annually for five years.

It was during this five-year period, when I was somewhere between the age of twenty and twenty-three, that I lost the Lord Jesus as the true goal of my life and became so highly engrossed in my college career—getting my degrees in piano.

I know now why all these religious, ritualized experiences were not as truly meaningful as the baptism of the Holy Spirit. It is far more meaningful when God moves upon man, than when man merely turns on his own and does something that he thinks is of God. "For by grace are ye saved through faith; and that not of yourselves: it is the gift of God: **Not of works** lest any man should boast" (Ephesians 2:8-9).

From the time I received the baptism of the Holy Spirit in 1973, the Lord has surely been working with me. He has drawn me and my family closer to Him day by day. I know that we have a long way to go, but at least God knows that we are willing to live our lives for Him. Daily, we ask Him to be Lord of our lives.

Maybe it's because of my artistic nature that my spirit cries out for freedom in a direct, natural and spontaneous relationship with God. The Lord knows how to fulfill our needs—even those of our personality. He led us to a Full Gospel Charismatic Church, where we can truly worship Him openly, in the spirit and in truth. The body of Christ here has certainly undergirded me and my family in every way, spiritually and physically, whenever there was a need. We feel very honored to belong to a church that ministers Jesus. I not only find Jesus in our church, but I feel comfortable coming into His presence amidst the members of His body.

"They will know we are Christians by our love. . . ." These words are so meaningful. In our church we try, as Christians, to love each other—no matter what has been in your past. Where you come from doesn't matter. In other words, no one holds my past against me. Jesus loved the sinner, not the sin; but He did go out of His way to minister to the sinner. "How think ye? if a man have an hundred sheep, and one of them be gone astray, doth he not leave the ninety and nine, and goeth into the mountains, and seeketh that which is gone astray? And if so be that he find it, verily I say unto you, he rejoiceth more of that sheep, than of the ninety and nine which went not astray" (Matthew 18:12-13).

12
1 + 1 = 3

"How would you like swimming through that big whale's mouth?" I asked Paul as the two of us glanced through his new *Jonah and the Whale* color book.

He really startled me with the reply, "Well, if I had been Jonah I would have gone to Nineveh!"

Whew! I was speechless at his wise answer which presupposed a pretty thorough understanding of that Bible story for a five-year-old. How interesting it would be to know everything that went on inside his mind and what made this little boy project such an answer. When I was five years old I didn't even know anything about Jonah.

This incident is just typical of many such precious episodes in the life of our J. Paul (Joseph Paul), more commonly known as Paul. He is our firstborn and so dear to us. The Lord has had His hand on Paul from the beginning. He constantly amazes us with the deep spiritual understanding that he has. One doesn't expect this in a child so young.

Paul's first four years were spent as an only child. Day by day as we experienced the treasured moments of rearing him, our desire for another child grew and grew. We didn't think it would be possible for us to have another child of our own. We prayed for the Lord to show us what to do. My feelings leaned heavily toward adopting an underprivileged child. However, we were not really sure which direction to take on this either.

One evening at the weekly prayer meeting held in our home, I sat in the "prayer chair" and asked for those present to pray and agree with us that God would give us another child, and that He would show us which route to take in the adoption. "And it shall come to pass, that before they call, I will answer; and while they are yet speaking, I will hear" (Isaiah 65:24).

We were first led to share our desire with our pastor. We thought that maybe since our church had a mission in Mexico that we might be able to adopt an orphan from there. We told him of our idea, but he related that that would be impossible due to Mexican government regulations. Our meeting with him seemed fruitless, but it really wasn't. God had led us to take a step in the right direction. From then on, our pastor knew of our intense desire for another child and the missing links in the chain, so to speak, were being put together by the Almighty to make our desire come true. Later, he was able to relate this desire that we had to a missionary woman who was directly connected with an orphanage in Seoul, Korea.

Just a few months later, she spoke at our church and I felt the Holy Spirit tugging at my heartstrings as she spoke about helping some American families adopt orphans from the Orient. I approached her after the service and asked if she could get us a baby or a small child. Her answer was, "Oh, you're the ones!"

Our pastor had already talked with her about us wanting to adopt a child. That was the beginning of a waiting period of only nine months—incredible in two ways: it matched the waiting period of natural motherhood, and it was an incredibly short wait for an adoption procedure.

The months we waited were busily spent. I was teaching school again, and we were enrolled in a Bible Foundation class which we pursued vigorously. The time just seemed to flow by very quickly. About the time all the papers were completed on the adoption, I suspected "something unexpected" happening to me physically. I went to my obstetrician, and after the examination his eyebrows and tone of voice depicted surprise. "Looks like about two and a half months!" he said.

So, we found ourselves preparing for two arrivals, one via Japan Air Lines and the other on the wings of a stork. I certainly do thank God that they both didn't arrive at the same time—though this is just another example of God's perfect timing.

I was on my face many times before the Lord while waiting for both of these arrivals. One time in particular, when praying in the front bedroom, the Lord gave me such a surge of love for my little child who was coming from the Orient. It was like that love was all of a sudden planted in my heart for him even though I had not been able to see or touch him, yet. I believe God granted me this love because we had really moved out in faith in seeking this child. We asked the Lord to provide the money if He wanted us to have him, and He did, quite to our surprise. Mother gave us a $1,000 check without us asking her. We accepted this as confirmation that God wanted us to adopt this child.

We left it up to the Lord as to which child to send us. We didn't even specify that it had to be a boy or a girl. We left the whole thing in God's hands, knowing that His choice would be His perfect will for our family. Only He would know which child would fit into our family the best. Shortly after this prayer was said, we received a picture and a brief description of the little boy we were getting from our missionary friend. I prayed and prayed for his safety while traveling to us. He and another little six-year-old boy were going to fly directly from Seoul, Korea, to us in Shreveport, all by themselves, with only a stewardess to escort them. What a frightful experience for two little six-year-olds—making that long trip over here to this strange land. Many times while I was waiting for his arrival, I was led to pray for all the people in the Orient, especially the Chinese, Japanese, and the Koreans.

Finally, Kim Yong Sik, a precious little Korean boy arrived at our home on March 10, 1976. Even though he could not speak a word of English, he and Paul "hit if off" right from the start, in more ways than one, if you know what I mean. There is certainly no language barrier with children.

Speaking of "hitting it off," shortly after Yong Sik arrived, Paul approached him from behind, encircled him with his arms to love him. Much to Paul's surprise, he received the most awful Karate chop blow from Yong Sik that one could imagine. You see, in Korea, he lived with fifty or so other boys who daily fought among themselves, even for their food. So, when Paul grabbed him to love him, he probably thought that he was being attacked for some possession of his. Needless to say, Paul learned in a hurry to be very cautious around his new brother—for a while, anyway.

Tim (renamed by us—Timothy Yong McLeod) was so little when he came to us at the age of six. He didn't look any more than four years old. Paul was three years younger than he, but Paul was taller. In the first year that he was here he grew seven inches!!

The first two or three months with Tim were hard. I'm sure that for him the adjustment was traumatic, especially for a child. We did try to abide completely by the principles of discipline and love as given in God's Word. I'm not saying we didn't make any mistakes. I know that often my temper got the best of me. I was five months pregnant when Tim arrived and feeling somewhat badly. I gave in to myself and sometimes took it out on him at the least infringement of a rule, that in reality, he probably didn't even understand. But God is so good. Tim just naturally came by a bad temper and wanted everything his way. So our strictness, tempered with much love, was used by the Lord to tame the wild spirit in him.

He adapted so well to his new environment that after just a few months, when our baby came, he was ready to go to Texas with Paul and stay for a short visit with Grandmother. He had forgotten all the Korean language by then, which is a shame, but there was no one to speak it with him. It only took him three months to understand and speak English.

All three of our children are very precious to us in their own way. Tim may not be our own flesh and blood but the lineage he bears from us is the love for him that God gave us—that love that sought after him and waited for him. It is a very special kind of love.

Kim Yong Sik, age 6. Photo taken in Korea.

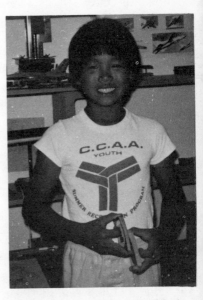

Tim, now a fully naturalized U.S. citizen.

13
Caesarean Trauma

"Everything will be all right, honey, just phone some people to pray," I whispered faintly as I grabbed for Richard's hand. They were wheeling me into surgery for the second time that morning.

The first surgery was expected and planned and seemed to go off like clockwork. I remember a lot of details because I was awake when Anne Marie was born. The anesthesiologist who had administered the spinal announced the Caesarean delivery of a beautiful baby girl. After a few minutes the pediatrician brought her around for me to see. I was audibly praising God for that baby girl. What a beautiful answer to prayer!

After the C-section, I was wheeled into the recovery room. At first everything seemed to be regular routine. But, after a little while, the nurse in charge looked worried. She kept pushing on my stomach every few minutes. I couldn't imagine why there was such a fuss about me. The problem was the uterus would not contract to its usual pear size as it should after birth. When it does not contract, its "spongy" consistency leaves blood vessels wide open, which causes uncontrollable bleeding. They tried to keep damp gauze over my eyes so I wouldn't see what was happening, but I wouldn't let them. The first unit of blood was started intravenously. Before it was all over, I had to have eight units of blood. I remember saying, "Please don't cover my eyes, it's all right, I'm not afraid." Vital signs were taken about every five minutes, as I was bordering on a state of shock from the loss of so much blood.

The hospital staff could not find my doctor right away. When he did arrive, I saw him beside my bed with a look of much concern on his face as he questioned the nurse, "How long has this been going on?" Then I again heard him say, "We'll have to go back to surgery and remove the uterus."

I smiled at him and nodded, "Yes," and peacefully drifted into semi-consciousness. I awoke again in a few minutes and asked if I could see my husband before going back into surgery.

During the time all of this was going on, the nurse in charge of the nursery could not figure out why no one had been to see the McLeod baby. She knew Mr. McLeod was in the hospital. She had seen him on the floor earlier. After several hours, word finally came from surgery that Mrs. McLeod was returning to the floor but was listed as critical and that she had undergone two consecutive surgeries.

The second surgery was extremely crucial. My condition was very critical on the operating table, due to hemorrhagic shock. The anesthesiologist told my doctor to do only the surgery that was absolutely necessary and to rush with that. I have learned since that the most crucial thing was that they had to put me under anesthesia twice within so short a time. The doctor was forced to abandon the ordinary hysterectomy procedure, as he only had time to remove the uterus, part of the cervix, and one ovary, which was removed because it had a tumor on it.

The doctor was somewhat skeptical about my prognosis because he thought I would have bad bleeding complications due to the partial cervix that he did not remove. But, several weeks later, upon examination at the doctor's office, he explained that he couldn't understand it—there was no cervical tissue in my body. The doctor was forced to do only a partial job—but the Lord healed me perfectly—leaving nothing undone.

During the time I spent in the hospital recovering, and especially those days I was in critical condition, I just have to say those were precious days. Most of me had been "wiped out" and the Lord really did move in. There were no stumbling blocks to His work. He ministered to me in such a beautiful way that I would not take anything for those moments.

Those around me thought I was really suffering, when in fact, I was really receiving a blessing from the Lord. It was a time of spiritual growth. The first thing I remembered was hearing the most beautiful music—a tremendous throng singing, "The Lord is my light and my salvation; whom shall I fear?" (Psalm 27:1), alternating with the "Alleluia" that we sing. I told my husband about this experience and he changed his mind about bringing me tapes to listen to. Maybe I was dreaming, but anyway the Lord was doing it much better than any tapes could.

I also heard in a prophecy words very similar to Psalm 71:18. God told me that He would let me live to tell the new generation all the wondrous things that He had done for me. How then could I help recovering quickly, with such a ministry going on in my spirit? To everyone's amazement, on the third day after surgery, I was sitting up and visiting with Mother and other friends from out of town.

The night before my surgery, I had been a little fidgety. I couldn't seem to settle down. I watched a dumb movie in my hospital room about some unfortunate tragedy occurring in a hospital—of all things. But the night before that when I was still at home, Richard took the two boys to the movie and gave me an evening at home by myself. So I had about three hours before the Lord, alone. I began my "mini-retreat" by playing worship songs to the Lord on the piano and singing my heart out to Jesus. I cried and played and sang many verses of many songs. Somehow, I sensed a little trouble to come—connected with the birth of our baby. I prayed diligently that no matter what, the baby would be normal and healthy. I praised the Lord for His love and mercy, and for forgiveness of all my wrongdoings, and having again put me in right standing with Him. The time went by in a hurry but I remember that before the "boys" got back home, I had received a complete peace in my spirit. I knew that somehow everything would be all right.

Anne Marie weighed seven pounds and eleven ounces—a very plump, healthy baby. Because I had been so critical for a few days, Richard spent two nights on a cot in my room. I didn't get to see Anne Marie much the first few days, but after that Richard and I took turns feeding her the bottle, which was a real joy to both of us.

God's blessings mounted as I continued to recover. I was a little put out with the doctor, though, when he would not release me on our wedding anniversary as planned. He kept me one day longer because I had been so sick. The day of our anniversary I got the surprise of my life. Richard showed up at my hospital room with two plates from our best china, and two of our beautiful crystal glasses that we had gotten for our wedding. He had bought a red rose in a stem vase. After making a beautiful place setting for the two of us in my hospital room, in he came with steaming-hot cashew chicken from a swanky restaurant. It was not only delightful for me, but his romantic gestures tugged at all the nurses' heartstrings, too.

The devil didn't like it a bit that we all had been so blessed by the Lord during this time which looked like so much suffering to the world. So, after Anne Marie and I got home he kept after me for about a month—trying to steal my healing. I jaundiced badly, and evidently had a bad kidney infection. One thing led to another. I will not glorify the devil by even mentioning all the symptoms he tried to put on me. I just kept turning to Jesus. Sometimes I was so weak and sick that all I could get out was His holy name. I just repeated, "Jesus, Jesus. . . ." I slowly recovered and was able to seek the Lord again in His holy Word. To this day it is His Word that keeps me going. The psalmist said it so well: "Thy word is a lamp unto my feet, and a light unto my path" (Psalm 119:105).

Anne Marie, age 3. This is one mother-daughter relationship that I hope will never be broken.

14
Love Chasteneth

" . . . *that ye should turn from these vanities unto the living God, which made heaven and earth, and the sea, and all things that are therein*" (Acts 14:15b).

The early morning sun streamed through the small oval window as the big 747 made its way over France. Four or five hours east lay our longed-for destination: Tel Aviv, Israel.

Richard and I hadn't rested much on the first eighteen hours of the trip. Our anticipation was too great because we knew the Lord had some great blessings in store for us as we visited our Lord and Saviour's homeland, the very terrain where He had set foot while on this earth. Nevertheless, I seemed a little relaxed now, as I glanced at my watch to check on the time change I would have to make. I remembered that I had to set my watch ahead seven hours. While doing this, a fleeting glance at my hands sent a panic through my entire system: my wedding rings!! They were not on my finger and somehow, right then, I knew I would never see them again. I sat very still, staging a relaxed composure, while on the inside I was frantically trying to decide what to do first. I didn't want to tell Richard until I was sure that they were missing. I checked my purse and then walked to the restroom where I had taken my rings off to wash my hands. My heart sank even further. But I really wasn't surprised to find that they were not there. Then I walked further back on the plane and approached our assistant pastor and some of our tour group. I asked them to pray with me that the Holy Spirit would touch the heart of whomever took my rings and that they would turn them in to the airline personnel.

Everyone in that small prayer circle sensed immediately that this careless mistake I had made could be a very upsetting factor that the devil could use to block some of the blessings my husband and I were to receive in the Holy Land.

An hour or so elapsed, and the tension in me mounted. I would have to tell Richard, and I knew how hurt and upset he would be. Finally, I mustered enough courage to tell him. He was so upset that he couldn't even answer me. What upset me the most, though, far more than losing my rings, was when I saw a big tear form in the corner of Richard's eye.

About that time our tour host, a good friend and Sunday school teacher from our church, came to pray with us. I shared with him that the devil was really using this to get us upset. As soon as I got those words out, I began to sob uncontrollably. *Hadn't I made enough mistakes, Lord? Why this?* After this friend prayed with us, a calm settled in my spirit and over Richard. The Lord God was gracious to point out to us that our love was bigger than any set of rings, and that earthly treasures don't matter anyhow. This is really a tough lesson to learn sometimes.

We landed in Tel Aviv, were bussed to Jerusalem, and by the time we had checked into our hotel, it was as if the whole incident never happened. The lesson we learned purged our hearts just a little bit cleaner, in preparation to receive those good things the Lord had in store for us. I suppose that this could be taken as a good sign that we were still growing in the Lord.

On the second day in Jerusalem we toured the Shepherd's Fields in Bethlehem, and then visited a small store in Bethlehem where Richard bought a gold wedding band for me. That ring has a very special significance for me, because while wearing it, two days later, we renewed our wedding vows at the garden tomb where the burial and resurrection of Jesus took place. That was such a moving ceremony. It was a beautiful summer day. Another tour group was singing in the background, and doves were cooing as all the couples on our tour group solemnly pledged their love and devotion again to their spouses. Those moments meant more to me than when we were first married. I felt much cleaner spiritually, and the vows we pledged seemed so much more sincere. For now we were walking closer to God, had a personal relationship with His Son, Jesus, and the whole thing seemed better even if outwardly our wedding several years earlier had more pomp and flourish.

Going to Israel is one of the greatest blessings that God can give to anyone. Visiting the places where Jesus walked, worked miracles, and died on the cross makes those things so real. The whole plan of God's salvation unfolds concretely right before your eyes. It probably affects everyone differently as to where they are in their walk with God, at the time when they go to these sacred places. But it is such a meaningful experience. I would love to go back as often as I could. I've been told that you leave a part of your heart in Jerusalem—I know this is true.

15
No Other Gods!

For a while after I was filled with God's Holy Spirit, I thought life was going to be a breezy waft into the heavenlies. But shortly thereafter I discovered my *fleshly counterpart:* the *world* and *old slew foot* were still around. Just because a person is a Spirit-filled Christian, this doesn't mean that he or she is immune to the attacks of Satan.

For several years now I have had a deep inner longing to grow closer and closer to the Lord, and have wanted the same for my family. This inner yearning has been so sincere and yet, I know that we all have a long way to go; there is still a lot of room for growth. A few years ago a Christian talk show had built a new prayer chapel and was asking for prayer requests to be sent in by their partners (people like us who supported them each month). These requests were placed in the prayer chapel and prayed over daily. Well, at the top of my list that I sent in, I put this request: that God would help my family to seek Him first in everything we did.

I really meant this. However, my sincerity on a slip of paper was not all the insurance I needed to make my continuous climb up the ladder to perfect a certain thing. I was reading my Bible and praying every day, or almost every day—for it is so easy to get caught up in the every-day activities of making a living and raising a family. The devil has complicated our lives to the extent that it gets very hard to put God first or even think about Him at times, especially when worldly pressures get tough. But, we cannot give up trying. We must keep on "keeping on."

I know from personal experience that if we let down our spiritual guard, old slew foot projects into us the very temptation that penetrates to our weakest spot in the flesh. And almost before we know it, we have abandoned our first love—Jesus—for a sordid counterfeit, some other god. For we begin seeking someone or something instead of Jesus. We pray less; read the Bible less; we lose our perspective of created things and their relation to the Godhead: our Creator. We lose our sense of responsibility. In other words, we really mess things up.

Whenever we have lost our "priority lineup" we can count on the fact that we have reached an unhealthy imbalance. Something is out of place, and this snowballs into greater problems, like loopholes in the priority scheme. Someone is being neglected or maybe even left out. Our priority lineup should be:

> God . . . first
> mate . . . second
> children . . . third
> job . . . fourth
> others . . . fifth

In almost every case, one or more of the top three categories are affected the most. But no matter which one suffers, it affects our relationship with God—because we are not moving in His will for our lives. When we forsake our "priority lineup" for something else, we are in essence worshipping another god.

Some make **money** a god.
Some make **success** a god.
Some make **their stomachs** a god.
Some make **another person** a god.
Some make **television** a god.
Some make **sports** a god.
Some make **alcohol** a god.

This list could go on and on, *ad nauseam*. Matthew 6:24 says: "No man can serve two masters: for either he will hate the one, and love the other; or else he will hold to the one, and despise the other. Ye cannot serve God and mammon."

Not too long ago, I got caught in this trap of getting my priorities mixed up. It didn't happen over night. Little by little, I let something creep in and almost control me to the point of destruction. I became obsessed with my false god. It was all I could think about, even to the point where I had let it drive away my proper relationship with God, my husband and my family. But God loves me so much that He "zapped" me back to my senses. He allowed some cruelty of others to bring me to my knees and seek forgiveness. I went to a pastor and his wife for some counseling and they discerned some spirits from which I needed deliverance. Yes, even Spirit-filled believers can need deliverance from oppressions, if they fall away from God. I have seen this happen to several people. After that day, when I was delivered, I felt an unbearable weight was lifted from my shoulders. I was able to pray again and felt my spirit returning to its first love—Jesus.

One important thing through this ordeal was that I knew I was doing wrong, and was able to ask some Christian friends to pray for me, even though I couldn't seem to touch God with my prayers. Still other friends of mine had a burden to pray for me, and I hadn't even asked them. Oh, the beauty of the ministry of the "body of Christ." I wanted to get straightened out, but my own efforts seemed fruitless. Later, I found that at least twelve people were bombarding heaven for me, and finally God laid the axe to the very root of the problem and a spiritual surgery took place. I was delivered, freed, and most of all, forgiven and washed again with the precious blood of Jesus. How God must love me!

One major thing I have learned through all of this is that it doesn't matter whether other people forgive your failures. If they can't forgive you, that is between them and God. If you are forgiven by God, and with His grace have mended your ways, you need not be plagued about the response of other people.

"Behold **God is my salvation;** I will trust and not be afraid: for the Lord Jehovah is my strength and my song; he also is become my salvation" (Isaiah 12:2).

" . . . for the strength of evil men shall be broken, **but the Lord takes care of those he has forgiven**" (Psalm 37:17, LB).

"The steps of good men are directed by the Lord. He delights in each step they take. If they fall it isn't fatal, for the Lord holds them with his hand" (Psalm 37:23-24, LB).

I am not saying that it is all right to seek other gods, and that God will simply rescue you if you do. What I am saying is that we must be very careful in our relationship with the Lord. He wants first place in the "priority lineup." But, He is a gentleman, and will step aside if we want Him to. However, this is very dangerous ground upon which to tread. One wrong move can ruin the happiness of many lives. We need to seek God first every day of our lives so that He will keep us with His divine providence.

"Thou hast also given me the shield of thy salvation: and thy right hand hath holden me up, and thy gentleness hath made me great" (Psalm 18:35).

"Fear thou not; for I am with thee: be not dismayed; for I am thy God: I will strengthen thee: yea, I will help thee; yea, I will uphold thee with the right hand of my righteousness" (Isaiah 41:10).

"For the Lord loveth judgment, and forsaketh not His saints; they are preserved for ever: but the seed of the wicked shall be cut off" (Psalm 37:28).

When things go a little wrong in our home, as they do in any marriage here on earth, I hope I will always have this special insight and remember that my nature and background has caused me to crave an inordinate amount of love that no man, however perfect, can fulfill. God alone will fulfill all the aspects of a true lover, here and now as much as we let Him, and perfectly for all eternity. Meanwhile, I need to forget about my personal needs and work toward filling the needs of those around me, first of all my husband, and then my children, and then the brothers and sisters God directs across my path.

16
Ministry of the Body of Christ

Everyone had arrived for our backyard picnic. We sat down to the covered-dish feast that had been prepared by various members of our home prayer group. We had invited our assistant pastor and his wife and called on him to ask God's blessing on our food. The food was delicious, but the fellowship we had with our Christian friends was even better. After the meal, we sat around in the back yard singing Scripture songs, accompanied by a guitar.

Only one thing marred the almost perfect joy of the evening. One of our most faithful prayer group members, upon arriving that evening, had disclosed the results of her recent physical examination. The doctors had found a very large tumor in her colon, which would have to be removed. After eating, our pastor anointed her with oil and we prayed—believing that God was going to give her a thorough healing.

The following week she had her surgery. They found a very fast-growing cancer which had already spread to some other organs. This was on a Tuesday. On Friday we had our regular prayer meeting, and the most wonderful thing was inaugurated at that meeting. After learning the plight of our sister and the lean chances of survival the doctors gave her, someone decided that we should fast and pray for her healing. It was only a suggestion. As soon as it was mentioned, though, others confirmed that they felt the same way. There were thirteen people at our home that evening, and immediately a unanimous affirmation was given to this suggestion. You can't tell me that the love of Jesus that unites the members of His body didn't prompt this gesture! We decided to go on a seven-day fast, followed by communion on the last day. I have never felt such a unity among believers as I did during those seven days.

Our sister recuperated slowly, and began the follow-up treatment for cancer: chemotherapy. She underwent all the usual treatment and tests that a cancer patient has to endure for about a year after surgery. When the year was over the doctors could not find any more cancer anywhere in her body. Semi-annual tests have proven negative since that time. This was almost five years ago. Even though our prayer groups had to disband for several reasons, and I don't see her much any more, I still see her out walking in the neighborhood. She is a picture of health.

My whole point in mentioning this is the importance of the body of Christ and our membership and fellowship in it.

Since my conversion and baptism in the Holy Spirit, the Lord has given us a new circle of friends—good Christian friends. Good Christian friends will stand by you, no matter what. Worldly friends have a way of disappearing when the going gets tough. I don't know what I would have done if God hadn't placed exactly the right people around me when I needed them the most, to minister to me in a godly way. They know how to love you with the *agape* love, the love of Jesus. They love you when you're hurt and correct you, in love, if you need it. They know how to share when there is a need financially—or whatever the need is. They are patient in their love, while waiting for God to deal with you. Most of all, they will pray with you, intercede for you—even if it means fasting for you, or praying all night for you. They are always available if you need them—even at their own inconvenience.

If you have made yourself a member of the body of Christ, by your acceptance of Jesus as your Lord and Saviour, then you have joined the most important corporate body in this life and the next. I hasten to add, **even more important than the body of your natural family.**

I have had Christian friends call and say that God had given them a burden to pray for me, and that they had done that for several days at a time until the release from that burden would come into their spirit. Amazingly, these have always been times when I have needed those prayers the most.

You should be a member of a good Bible-believing church, and worship there faithfully. It is also important to join a home fellowship of believers—sometimes called a prayer group or prayer meeting. Many, if not all, personal needs can be taken care of at these more intimate meetings. It has become harder and harder to cope with living in today's world, but if we will seek the Lord first, and fellowship with believers, it is a whole lot easier. Hebrews 10:25 admonishes us: "Not forsaking the assembling of ourselves together, as the manner of some is; but exhorting one another: and so much the more, as you see the day approaching."

EPILOGUE

No sin, I don't care how big it is in the sight of the world, **is too big for God to forgive.** Second Chronicles 7:14 says: "If my people, which are called by my name, shall humble themselves, and pray, and seek my face, and turn from their wicked ways; then I will hear from heaven, and will forgive their sins, and will heal their land."

Some of us, like myself, whose Adamic nature is so filled with pride, are capable of putting on a pretty fancy facade. But, underneath, the same sins and temptations plague us as do the rest of humanity. Most of us just don't admit it.

This book is simply a very honest appraisal of some of my shortcomings and sins and how the Lord has rescued me from them. It was written to be a witness to others that **if we do love God and try to mend our ways, He is more than willing to forgive us,** and sometimes, more often than we care to admit. I feel I can truly quote the Psalmist David here, as if these were my own words, written by my own hand:

PSALM 51
(Living Bible)

(Written after Nathan the prophet had come to inform David of God's judgment against him because of his adultery with Bathsheba, and his murder of Uriah, her husband.)

O loving and kind God, have mercy. Have pity upon me and take away the awful stain of my transgressions.

Oh, wash me, cleanse me from this guilt. Let me be pure again.

For I admit my shameful deed—it haunts me day and night.

It is against you and you alone I have sinned, and did this terrible thing. You saw it all, and your sentence against me is just.

But I was born a sinner, yes, from the moment my mother conceived me.*

You deserve honesty from the heart; yes, utter sincerity and truthfulness. Oh, give me this wisdom.

Sprinkle me with the cleansing blood and I shall be clean again. Wash me and I shall be whiter than snow.

And after you have punished me, give me back my joy again.

Don't keep looking at my sins—erase them from your sight.

Create in me a new, clean heart, O God, filled with clean thoughts and right desires.

Don't toss me aside, banished forever from your presence. Don't take your Holy Spirit from me.

Restore to me again the joy of your salvation, and make me willing to obey you.

Then I will teach your ways to other sinners, and they — guilty like me — will repent and return to you.

Don't sentence me to death. O my God, you alone can rescue me. Then I will sing of your forgiveness, for my lips will be unsealed — oh, how I will praise you.

You don't want penance; if you did, how gladly I would do it! You aren't interested in offerings burned before you on the altar.

It is a broken spirit you want — remorse and penitence. A broken and a contrite heart, O God, you will not ignore.

And Lord, don't punish Israel (others) for my sins — help your people and protect Jerusalem.

And when my heart is right, then you will rejoice in the good that I do and in the bullocks I bring to sacrifice upon your altar.

All of my spiritual assurance is in the Lord Jesus, and, like David, I claim to be a man (woman) after God's own heart. Every Christian who seeks forgiveness can claim this gift of grace from God.